NO EXCUSES

NO EXCUSES

TURNING AROUND ONE OF BRITAIN'S TOUGHEST SCHOOLS

ALISON COLWELL

Biteback Publishing

For Pete Goddard

CONTENTS

Author's Note   xi

Preface   xv

Prologue   1

Chapter 1   2014–2015   5

Chapter 2   2015–2016   59

Chapter 3   2016–2017   109

Chapter 4   2017–2018   143

Chapter 5   2018–2019   183

An Open Letter to the Secretary of State for Education   215

Postscript: Summer 2020   223

Afterword   241

Acknowledgements   245

About the Author   249

You will teach them to fly but they will not fly your flight

You will teach them to dream but they will not dream your dream

You will teach them to live but they will not live your life

Nevertheless in every flight, in every dream, in every life
– the print of the way you taught them will remain.

– MOTHER TERESA

AUTHOR'S NOTE

I thought long and hard about writing this book, and indeed, I have asked myself many times why I did. I know why I didn't.

I most assuredly didn't write it to humiliate or embarrass parents (although if a parent doesn't love, nurture, nourish and care deeply for their child, they are certainly open to criticism). And I didn't write it to lament the dire state of education in this country or the terrible ordeal that is being a teacher. (Neither view could be further from the truth, as those of us lucky enough to work in this unique field know only too well. All around the country, schools – teachers – do wonderful, precious work, transforming lives and improving life chances.) And I certainly didn't do it to have a go at children. If you don't love children, you shouldn't be a parent and you definitely shouldn't be a teacher.

So, if there was a reason I wrote this book, it was to applaud the children who triumph against some very considerable odds, to shine a light on the extraordinary work that schools do, and to celebrate the joyous, special, unique and privileged role that is being a teacher.

This book was originally intended to be published anonymously, because this book is not, actually, about me or a certain school or specific children. This book is about teaching, education, courage, leadership, schools, passion, moral purpose and how the needs of children in a non-selective school can best be addressed. But for some reason known only to herself, the journalist who encouraged me, even urged me, to take an anonymous publishing deal then chose, a week before the original version of the book was going to print, to 'out' me in a Sunday newspaper.

Although the book is now published under my own name and draws on real events, the names, dates, personal information and other identifying details of pupils, parents and staff have been extensively changed to protect their privacy, and many episodes are based on an amalgamation of several different incidents and characters. This is a story of truth – focused on the issues and the challenges rather than the individuals – as opposed to a true story, and although the specific details have been changed, the essence of truth remains. As the book makes clear, one cannot please all the people all of the time and a number of the changes at the academy attracted controversy, but my book aims to show how such challenges can be met and how students' life chances and expectations can be improved.

The years covered in this book were the most challenging, most rewarding and most joyous five years of my career. I didn't get everything right, but I always, always did what I thought was right.

> *You can't go back and change the beginning, but you can start where you are and change the ending.*
>
> C. S. LEWIS

PREFACE

In 2014, I walked into a failing school. It was failing by every measure of a school. Of course, the results were dire – that year only 17 per cent of children attained five or more A* to C grades at GCSE (which was the measure at the time), or, as I prefer to describe it, 83 per cent of the children were failed by the school by not even getting that minimum qualification. But all the other trademarks of a failing school were also there. Appalling behaviour. Low standards and non-existent expectations. Uniform that was barely recognisable as one. A poor local reputation. Falling pupil numbers. A lack of any accountability. Dreadful teaching (although anyone would have struggled to teach in classrooms that were so chaotic and out of control). Acute difficulty in staff recruitment and retention (eighteen supply teachers working there at the time). A climate of fear and mistrust. In other words, poor leadership.

That school was closed by the Department for Education. Six months later, we opened as a new academy. We had sky-high expectations. We had strict and clear rules, which we enforced consistently. We had from day one a 'no excuses' culture and a focus on aspiration and excellence. I sacked teachers who didn't want things to improve – or worse, didn't believe that they could – and recruited young talent whose teaching made me cry with joy. Three years later we got inspected by Ofsted and were judged 'Good' across the board. During the feedback, the lead HMI (Her Majesty's Inspector) said to me that to have built the school we had, out of what we took on, in the area where we did, took 'exceptional leadership'.

But not everyone was supportive, and the loudest, angriest voices were from some of the parents who did not agree with the approach we took, despite the outcomes we secured. Having worked for twenty-two years in education, and predominantly in challenging schools, this was to be the toughest role I ever undertook. I was sworn at and threatened. We dealt with a fierce backlash from the parents when we sent children home for not wearing the correct uniform. We held same-day detentions for poor behaviour and had to battle parents coming into the school and physically removing their child from the detention room, in front of the staff and the rest of the children. We frequently called the police to remove aggressive parents from the school. I heard countless stories of children's lives that broke my heart, while I remained steadfast in my resolve to hold the line against their behaviour.

But throughout, I remained – and remain – utterly convinced that teaching is the noblest, the most joyous and the most rewarding job in the world. I loved going to work, I loved the children and I loved the very many wonderful staff I was able to recruit and develop in my role – conductor of the orchestra. We made mistakes but we learnt and moved on, and building our successful school is my proudest achievement.

This is that story.

PROLOGUE

There are a lot of faces in the hall in front of me. Most of them are scowling, sullen, bored. Many are also looking at their phones. It doesn't bode well. I look down at my creased speech, an unnecessary aid, given that I have rehearsed this a hundred times in my head, but it serves as a comfort blanket of sorts. I clear my throat and begin.

'Parents and local families, thank you for coming along here this evening. I hope over the next twenty minutes or so to lay out for you the vision I have of the new school, of what it will be like, how it will feel, and what we want it to do for the young people in this community, a community that for too long now has been poorly served and its children disadvantaged by the school we are currently standing in.'

A phone goes off. It's in the front row. I risk a frown. The owner, oblivious, answers it, his speech audible: 'Can't speak now, mate, at the school, listening to this new woman, going to be interesting. Nothing wrong with the old school in my view, or the old head.' A pause and a laugh. Looks up at me. 'Yeah, nice tits, but all trussed up in a suit!' Hangs up. Stares at me, defiantly.

I swallow and continue. 'Last summer a mere 17 per cent of students in this school achieved five A* to C grades, although I hesitate even to use the word "achieve", since what that really means is over three quarters of the young people who went to this school, Castlecliffe, failed even to gain that lowest of benchmarks. Or rather, they didn't fail – they were failed.

'I don't want to criticise the past regime, I don't want ever to criticise those in the teaching profession – there are professions far worthier of insult – but that school is closing; that school will end on 31 August of this year. A lot of you have said to me, "Oh yes, you're changing your name, aren't you?" Let me be really clear. This is not a name change. This is not a rebranding. That school is closing. We are opening a new school. It may be in the same building, with the same children and in the heart of the same community. But we are a new school. We have a very different vision, a very different aspiration, and things will be *very* different.' I glare at Mr Mobile. To be fair, he is now looking at my face.

'I have a very clear vision for the Lunsford Academy. Put simply, it is to become the number one school of *choice* in the local community. It will be a school characterised by outstanding teaching, as good as in any other school, be they comprehensive or grammar. It will be an over-subscribed school that children walk to, with their friends, where they *enjoy* coming, and a school of which they feel *proud*. It will be calm, orderly and welcoming. It will be a school where children leave the stresses and difficulties of the outside world at the gate. My vision is of an outstanding school, characterised by high aspirations, academic excellence and exemplary behaviour, but where alongside the firm discipline there is a strong current of care, encouragement and reward. And as well as achieving the highest qualifications they can, I want our students to fulfil all their potential, academic and personal, sporting and musical, creative and artistic. We want them to leave school as well-rounded, confident young people, with an awareness of the wider world and a desire and ambition to play an active part in it.

'The Lunsford Academy will have at its core outstanding teaching, lessons that the students go home and talk about, excitedly, and can't wait to come to school the next day, because school is interesting, challenging and fun. We must and we will build on that innate enthusiasm and motivation children have as they leave Year 6, and be absolutely determined there will be no dip in progress, but rather a heightened sense of excitement about learning. I want no child, of any ability, ever, to be able to say, "I'm bored."

'Finally, our academy will be an inclusive one, welcoming children of all abilities. I have always been driven by my passionate belief that with a cocktail of outstanding teaching, effective management and inspirational leadership, all schools can have an impact independent of neighbourhood. Deprivation does not, and must not, determine destiny.'

I sit down. There is a ripple of applause. It's a start. I look at Mr Mobile. He's definitely not looking at my face.

CHAPTER 1

2014–2015

'The danger for most of us is not that we aim too high and miss
our goals, but that we aim too low and reach them.'
– MICHELANGELO

We opened as the new academy in September 2014. Despite having laid out our stall, having explained and described our ambition, spelled out the rules, having made it crystal clear what we would and wouldn't accept, explained the Daily Detention that would run for those who broke the rules, we girded our loins for what we thought would be an inevitable onslaught. I still recall that first day, standing in the newly painted reception with the rest of the senior team, seeing smartly dressed student after smartly dressed student trot through, some looking nervous, many looking proud, a few looking very ill at ease. It was an uplifting moment. But, of course, there were going to be the exceptions and the resistance. Quite a lot, in fact.

MONDAY 1 SEPTEMBER 2014

It is a grey and damp morning. First day of the new academy. We stand in the reception greeting every student as they come through. A determined minority try, inevitably, to brazen it out, but we quietly direct them to one side: the students wearing trainers, the girls with plastered-on makeup, the one swaggering Year 11 whose audacity I have to admit a secret admiration for, as he actually arrives wearing jeans. In the end there are twenty-two. All have a phone call made to a parent, a letter given to them as they are redirected back home to change.

Mr Thompson, a parent, charges in and confronts me. 'What the fuck are you doing?' The last few students sitting in reception awaiting calls home look a mixture of embarrassed and excited. I politely reiterate (what I feel like I have been saying for the last six months): we have a uniform, we expect it to be adhered to, we have explained this for some time now and in fact every single pupil has been provided with an entirely new set, including the PE kit. Mr Thompson is not giving up, his son Troy standing by his side grinning defiantly at me. 'What fucking difference does it make? You are a fucking stupid cunt, and he ain't staying here.'

It will be the first of many such encounters.

TUESDAY 2 SEPTEMBER 2014

Chantelle's parents have gone to the local newspaper. 'Lunsford Academy parents seething as 45 pupils are sent home on their first day for incorrect uniform.' There is a picture of Chantelle in the article, looking as if butter wouldn't melt. This is a child who regularly truants, has repeatedly told teachers to fuck off, and it's fair to say is not going to be applying for the new prefect role any time soon. It is the first time I have ever seen her looking so smart, her (brand-new) uniform pristine and the camera focused on the shiny black shoes. (In our attempts to be crystal clear about uniform, to try to avoid the point-less splitting hairs about what is and isn't permitted, we have been utterly prescriptive, down to brand, down to heel height, down to material, down to the colour of the laces that adorn the shoes. Lacegate has started. Nobody will ever hate those bloody laces as much as I do.)

'All we care about is her schooling,' says Chantelle's mum, pi-ously, in the article. 'And we don't see how these red laces affect her education' – a line it's true to say I am going to become sick of. I want to say: why don't you send her to school every day then? Why don't you tell her it's not OK to swear at teachers? I read on.

'It's bloody ridiculous,' claims another, whose daughter we had turned around for multiple piercings and having a design-er handbag instead of a school bag. These parents, who don't support the rules, are especially angry because it was bitterly cold. 'You can't blame me for the weather,' the paper quotes me as saying, possibly a line that wasn't ever going to help things a great deal.

The paper starts an online poll: 'Should schools send pupils with the wrong uniform home?' Inevitably, during the day, the pollsters have prised themselves away from *Jeremy Kyle* and the votes have been streaming in, strongly against us. That evening,

I sit at home with my wine glass and get a bit fixated on it. In the end, 2,034 votes are cast, but with a narrow majority claiming the rules are unfair. I sense this is going to be quite a battle. And my wine intake is going to be on the up.

WEDNESDAY 3 SEPTEMBER 2014

A major tabloid has picked up the story: 'Over 40 pupils denied entry to school for breaking draconian head teacher's rigorous new uniform rules.' I am quoted as saying, 'I make no secret of our strict rules as it's my belief that they create the foundations upon which academic excellence is built.' And mother-of-four Maria Marshall is also quoted, describing me as 'a sergeant major. My daughter has to wear foundation and concealer to cover her extremely large pores. She's very self-conscious about them.'

But, the blessed British public being as we are, it all starts to go rather well. In the end, 1,753 comments are posted, the overwhelming majority of them positive.

'If only a minority were sent home, it would appear that the head has got it right – more schools should follow suit.'

'When will these precious princesses realise the world doesn't revolve around them and that part of education is to learn discipline, and understand and obey the rules?'

'Well done, ma'am, society has lost its standards, mainly due to there being too few heads like you. Keep up the good work!'

'Namby-pamby nonsense!'

'Excellent! Let's hope this head teacher is the mould for all those who just don't seem to care what the children do. Well done, gold star and go to the top of the class.'

'The head teacher is 100% correct. What part of the word "rule" do parents not understand?'

I sit back and sip my wine, smugly. It's fair to say that I am being lulled into a false sense of security.

THURSDAY 18 SEPTEMBER 2014

Email from David Jones, my Vice-Principal:

> Hi, Gilly Clarke's mum came in today to speak to Mrs Butler and in front of her, mum took Gilly's Saturday Detention letter, said this is what she thought of it and tore it into pieces, placed it on the reception desk, and said, 'You can stick that up your fucking arse.' So firstly, boss, I have a feeling Gilly will not be attending detention and second not sure if you want to ban her mum?

SATURDAY 20 SEPTEMBER 2014

Lunsford Locals is an open community Facebook group (although even my use of the word 'open' is misleading and suggests a level of understanding of Facebook that I don't have. I hate Facebook – and Twitter, Instagram, Snapchat, TikTok and every other ridiculous 'platform' that pulls our attention away from what's happening in real life. I have never had, nor will I ever have, an account, believing it should more aptly be named Boastbook, and seeing it as a significant contributor to poor mental health, online bullying and a serious decline in children's communication skills. We keep a watchful eye, however, on all of them). Lunsford Locals has apparently been going for some time; it is used to reminisce and research local history, as well as to promote community cohesion. Of late, however, it has taken to commenting on the school, and, inevitably, become an easy platform for our critics to slag us off from the safety of their sofas. There is a picture posted of the new uniform, and a discussion (of sorts) starts:

LR: I went to that school a few years ago, left just in time it seems! It makes me laugh, who do they think they are these people? The thing they don't get is this is a Lunsford secondary school, for goodness sake, not some posh place! [This comment depressingly encapsulates all the low aspirations and expectations that have contributed to Castlecliffe's decline.]

DH: I totally agree with you mate! It's Lunsford, case dismissed! LOL

OY: Anyone out there agree with me and my missus that the new blazer will make our kids look like Butlin's reps? I think we've got a new Stalin!

MK: The staff are crap as are the new rules. A name change won't change that. Listen you lot, don't get me wrong, I agree with clamping down on behaviour and wanting kids to have better exams but they r trying to take away their individuality!! Absolute farce.

DH: The rules r so extreme! Well bollox! And what's with the shoes thing, coloured laces aint gonna affect a child's learning!!! Fooking school!!

SW: Why don't all the staff follow the daft rules as well … they should set an example … you're not telling me that stuck up cow's hair is that colour, it's so dark and without a single grey hair, natural my arse! It's ok for her to be an individual but not our kids, stupid bitch.

• • •

Schools fail because of failed leadership. It really is that simple. A lack of accountability, ineffective systems, poor staff performance – all point to failure in leadership. Leadership, while a privilege (and to lead a school an honour) is hard. People look to you for the answers. You are under constant scrutiny. A leader can say what they like, but people will watch what they do. A wise school leader once told me: keep an eye always on your rear-view mirror; every single thing you do will be debated, analysed and interpreted (and misinterpreted).

In addition, education has become over-complicated. Standards are raised in school by a focus on the basics, a common-sense approach to everything, and the relentless, genuine pursuit of unwavering high standards in all things. Outstanding teachers, effective support staff, all held accountable, appropriately rewarded, valued and motivated, acting as excellent role models at all times. Inspiring lessons meticulously planned, engagingly delivered; clear rules strictly and consistently enforced. No lengthy documents that go unread, no pointless meetings, no misplaced energy but a relentless drive to ensure students attain. A decisive and strong head, who constantly walks the school, knows the students and operates fairly.

So one of the most important tasks I faced when I started was to appoint a new leadership team. I was very lucky: I found three wonderful young leaders who worked tirelessly with me from the beginning, standing quite literally by my side. I still remember reading the application from David, his CV a list of A*s at GCSE, four straight As at A level, a degree in maths from Cambridge. (I remember him later telling me that when he was born, 1985, David was the most common Christian name and Jones the most common surname – 'So I am quite common!' – but he certainly wasn't.) He wrote in his application:

My personal philosophy of education is influenced as much by my experience as a learner as by my experience as a teacher. I am fortunate to have enjoyed my school years, to have been academically challenged by my teachers and to have been inspired by their example. I was fiercely proud of my school and knew that I was a valued member of its community. I was supported in achieving my potential and was constantly expected to do so. These should be the minimum entitlements for all children and it is the duty of school leaders to ensure that they are achieved.

His words still, to this day, send a shiver down my spine.

'How do you handle the stress and pressure of the job?' I asked him at interview.

He shrugged cheerfully. 'I'm not a big fan of relaxation.' I knew the head of the school where he then worked; she had led the transition from a school almost identical to Castle-cliffe, with all the poor behaviour, low standards and parental opposition we were facing. David was in charge of improving behaviour there. I needed someone to do that at Lunsford, someone with steel, stamina and standards. I called my head friend up, asked her what David was like, beyond the impressive intellect.

'He's like no one else I've ever met. He's relentless, exceptionally talented, energetic, driven. Cares passionately about transforming children's life chances. He will really piss people off and get up their noses.' A lot of people were going to need that. I knew he was going to be a brilliant appointment.

MONDAY 29 SEPTEMBER 2014

Mrs Smith is very clear. 'I am not leaving until you give me the fucking phone back!' She looks across the table at me, her gaze steadfast but furious, her lip curled, sweat forming on her brow; she hates me even though she doesn't know me. Until today we hadn't even met. Yet she looks at me with pure, undiluted hatred.

Inwardly I sigh, and then: 'As you know, as I explained on the phone, we will be keeping Craig's phone for the rest of the term, as is clearly laid out in the behaviour policy. Which is on the website. Which you have a copy of. Which has remained unchanged since day one.' As you fucking well know, I add, but just to myself.

'You can't take it, it's theft, I'm getting the police up here. Tell 'er.' She glances at the man to her right – husband, boyfriend, father – I don't actually know, we weren't introduced as she stormed in here fifteen minutes previously, telling me she wasn't leaving without the phone, that she would cause havoc for me, that she was (obviously) going to the papers, slamming two phones down on the table. Not actually a shortage of phones in your household then, I wanted to say, but didn't, of course. Instead I just listen to the torrent of accusations and abuse, while mentally listing everything else I should be doing at this moment rather than sitting here, being abused, and sworn at, and threatened by the mother of the Year 9 pupil who hadn't heeded the rules, or more likely hadn't thought we'd enforce them, and had brazenly taken his phone out in French. Anyway, husband, boyfriend, father – whoever he is, he looks as though he wishes he was anywhere else other than where he is now, sitting in the formal meeting room of my school while his whoever-relative swears at me.

'It's not theft,' David, to my left, helpfully adds to the conversation. 'It's confiscation, under Section 91 of the Education and Inspections Act 2006.' He beams at her. He is well intentioned. He is trying to help, but at this point Mrs Smith's fury boils over. 'Don't you patronise me, you jumped-up little idiot, don't you go quoting the law and the rules to *me*. I don't give a fuck about them.

'I am getting the police, and I am not leaving without the fucking phone. Tell her, Mick.' She prods him, and at this moment it is hard to tell who she hates more: me, the Vice-Principal, or the useless whoever-relative who is by her side but clearly not on it. 'Nobody likes what you're doing here, everyone hates you and her.' A jabbing finger pointing at me lest anyone be under any illusion about whom she is talking.

'I don't actually think that's true, Mrs Smith. I actually think most people who care about education and raising standards and, in fact, their children, support what we are doing and the direction we are going. They support the changes we have made from what was a failing institution, failing your children, failing your community, and failing you. I think you'll find that Craig being without his phone for a few weeks will not kill him, it will in fact help him. And seeing as how your thirteen-year-old son has a reading age of six, which is indisputably holding him back and contributing to his chronically poor progress, and undoubtedly to the problems he is having concentrating in most lessons, it might be useful if you actually got him to read to you, a book, not a text or a website or a post, but a book, a proper one with paper pages, printed, and, trust me, that will be time well spent.'

But of course, I don't say this, I just think it, and what I actually say is: 'I am sorry you feel this way. You can collect the phone on the twenty-first of October. Until that time it will be kept securely in our safe, and if you are refusing to leave then I will.'

And I get up and walk out, leaving her sobbing and swearing and holding onto the table, while Mick shifts uncomfortably in his chair.

'Well done, we held the line,' David chirps cheerfully as we're walking down the stairs five minutes later, and I think, 'Yes, we did, but why on earth do we have to?'

TUESDAY 30 SEPTEMBER 2014

I receive an email from Jenny, our lovely receptionist:

I have taken three messages this morning for you.

1. Mrs Wilton – she's had no students here ever at this school but has read the newspaper article and she is very supportive – she says please stay strong, she wishes that there had been a strong leader at her children's school. She did not want to leave a telephone number.
2. Mr Davison from the North West on Sunday would like a telephone interview. He is supportive and wants to promote the school and the rules.
3. Mr Bennett from Wolverhampton says well done, you are doing a fantastic job. He wishes all schools had such a strong head teacher.

The kindness of random strangers never ceases to touch me, and motivates me to keep going; if only they knew.

THURSDAY 9 OCTOBER 2014

There is a great deal written about so-called 'superheads' and turning around failing schools. Much of what is written is wrong, especially the very notion of a superhead; it takes a whole village to raise a child. Of the millions of words that have been penned about school improvement (many of them by so-called experts and highly paid consultants who have never actually done it), I think it can be neatly reduced down to ten lessons.

Lesson 1: Firstly – and foremost – put the quality of teaching and learning centre stage. Make it the focus of everything: every conversation, every meeting, every policy. We would go on to create a culture of learning, of always looking to improve the craft that is teaching, learning from the best teachers and rooting out the weak. We always had a member of the senior team whose sole focus was teaching and learning, and who would rein us back if ever the hundreds of operational matters started to pull us away from our core purpose. We kept a database of every teacher, their strengths and weaknesses, that we would forensically pore over every week and find ways to support staff who were struggling.

Senior and middle leaders would be constantly in class-rooms, and we had an open-door policy so that a climate of openness and trust, of peer observation and ongoing improve-ment, was nurtured. Teachers would expect to be visited fre-quently, and would afterwards receive constructive, supportive feedback, and we did away with set-piece formal observations – most teachers can pull off a good lesson with advance warn-ing – but rather we concentrated on tasting the daily diet for every student, knowing that any teacher can have an off day but of more importance was the typicality of what went on in every classroom. We got feedback from students, and we filmed teachers in action so they could watch themselves after-wards and self-critique. We didn't send staff off on expensive training days (usually run by people who had long since left the classroom and of which the best bit was often the lunch) but trained in-house through peer observations, a culture of feedback, through sharing research, best practice, tricks and tips. We built collegiality and a shared sense of moral purpose.

We benefited from a number of exceptionally strong Teach First recruits, outstanding young graduates, intelligent, articulate, passionate about their subject and about tackling disadvantage, and we managed to retain many for longer than their two-year commitment, often by promoting to leadership roles where they could make an impact more widely across their subject. We put in strong support for new or trainee teachers, never forgetting how tough it is at the start for any teacher, in any school, let alone one with challenges, and ensured a constant supply of tissues, encouragement and constructive criticism. Every week, before school, we held 'Teaching, Tea and Toast Friday', where teachers shared tips and ideas, highlighted great practice they had seen that week, laughed, chatted and started the end of the week on a high rather than the tired low that can be so commonplace.

But teachers are born, not made (although we can all, always, improve), and ultimately we improved through attracting like-minded individuals, passionate about their subject and with sky-high standards and expectations. We attracted teachers who didn't think because a child struggles to read that they can't read but rather knew it was their job to make them read; teachers who didn't believe 'this child can't' but believed that all children can, and must; teachers who never settled for a dull PowerPoint*

---

* Having started my own teaching career with chalk, I remain convinced that the best resource in any classroom is the teacher and agree with the concept of the 'sage on the stage'. Of course, as the author George Couros said, 'Technology will not replace great teachers, but technology in the hands of great teachers can be transformational.' I did not want to be seen as a Luddite or backward-thinking (and I am slightly more tech-savvy than a friend of mine who once asked me, in all sincerity, 'You know when you send a fax, when the people the other end receive it – is it the same piece of paper?') So we aimed to use technology judiciously and wisely, but not excessively. We did, however, have occasional 'No Tech Week', when all teachers had to teach for the whole week without any technology. The most interesting outcome of this was the frequency with which staff, especially younger teachers, who had admitted to anxiety at the prospect of it, said they felt liberated and had enjoyed their teaching more.

but rather inspired and excited and ignited through their passion and energy and skill.

• • •

I receive an email from a parent following a bout of necessary hiring and firing:

I write to you in utter desperation, firstly the maths department has fallen apart, plus when Bradley returned in September he knew his new science teacher was going to be crap so he refused to go into the lesson, which I don't blame him for I tell you, but then he only went and got doled out a detention! Then he finds out that his PE teacher has resigned, yet another one of his GCSE subjects! Now he has come home today and said his bloody English teacher is leaving too, what on earth is going on? These poor Year 11 students should not have to suffer all this turmoil at this vital point, I am out of my mind with worry, I just keep thinking, who will be next, surely not that lovely Mrs Byers? I expect an answer.

Yours faithfully, Mrs Wilcox.

I ping a short reply:

Dear Mrs Wilcox,

Please arrange a meeting time with me so I can explain everything to you. With respect, you don't know the full picture. Happy to meet you before school (I get in at 7) or after (I leave at 7).

• • •

I didn't always want to be a teacher. No, scratch that – I *never* wanted to be a teacher. I loved school, all of it: I was the girlie swot and the A-grade student. But there were no teachers in my family and it had never occurred to me that I might make a good one. At university, I wanted to be a journalist, and then a police officer – like a less glamorous Miss World contestant, I just knew I wanted to do a job that was interesting, helped people and made a difference to the world. I joined the Met and for four years was an officer in Peckham, south-east London, in what was then one of the most dangerous and deprived parts of the city. It was hard, often frightening, and being a female officer in the '80s was, to say the least, a challenge. I still remember the detective chief inspector, in my first meeting, asking me lasciviously if I was on the pill in front of all the other (male) new recruits. Increasingly I felt I didn't fit. A friend who had gone into teaching used to talk about his work and he practically glowed. His eyes would shine as he talked about the children and the rewards. I watched *Dead Poets Society* and handed in my notice.

MONDAY 13 OCTOBER 2014
I update my website blog:

As I think you are aware – and certainly I have received a lot of support from you on this – we do not want students (girls in particular) bringing bags such as handbags that are simply too small and are not appropriate. We take, as with all things, a common-sense approach to this and the bags shown in the slides at the parent information sessions were merely a guide.

We want anything worn in the hair to be discreet, i.e. not too large and in a plain colour such as white, blue or black. Again, a common-sense approach is taken.

And finally, I have been inundated with emails and messages of support from parents and carers who are fully supportive of our strict stance on uniform, in line with that taken by all good and outstanding schools. Thank you. If in any doubt over an item, please contact us – as frequently stated, we want to work in partnership on all things so as to secure our shared aim of an excellent education for your child.

TUESDAY 14 OCTOBER 2014

Charles Kent is a history teacher. He joined Castlecliffe as one of the country's Teach First Ambassadors, the national scheme set up to try to attract high-calibre graduates into teaching. To be fair, it has a strong moral purpose at its heart and a lot of driven and intelligent young people among its applicants, drawn by the lure of working in disadvantaged schools, turning around young lives and having troubled and troublesome young people meekly eating out of their hands and hanging on their every word. Of course, in reality, after spending six weeks over their graduation summer on a 'baptism of fire' crash course in teaching, their initial laudable and genuine enthusiasm can get a little dented. During this time they are faced with the reality of trying to teach, often in poorly run schools in disadvantaged communities (where teachers are most urgently needed) and where, in the absence of strong leadership, sky-high expectations and a no-nonsense approach to discipline, even the most experienced of teachers will struggle. For these pups, it is often a blood bath. Charles has spoken to me about how he frequently used to think about just giving up during his first year (Teach Firsters are expected to spend at least two years in a school). He is one of my most enthusiastic and supportive members of staff, now that he's finally able to see a light at the end of the tunnel and has the opportunity to do what he always wanted to do: learn how to teach, and not how to fire-fight. I love being in his classroom; his combination of Prince Charming good looks, public school voice, passion for history and easy manner make him popular and engaging. He's also a sorely needed father figure and role model that so many (of our boys in particular) lack. Keeping him in the school is as much my priority as keeping all the children who challenge us. I make him the Subject Leader for History as money-where-mouth-is evidence of my belief and faith in him.

THURSDAY 16 OCTOBER 2014

I am on morning gate duty. Cheryl marches defiantly towards me, nose stud resplendent. Cheryl is one of the more challenging students in Year 8. ('Challenging' is such a wonderful euphemism, used the teaching world over. It's a useful shortcut for when teachers really want to say rude, argumentative, dis-respectful, stroppy, aggressive, disruptive and, clearly, badly brought up.)

'Take that out, please.' I smile cheerfully, holding out my hand.

She scowls. 'My dad paid thirty quid for that and you ain't having it.'

'I am sorry that your dad paid thirty pounds to break our rules, but you will still hand it over,' I reply, at which she turns on her heel and heads off, to what will no doubt be another week or so of unauthorised absence, and which will further hurt our attendance figures.

SATURDAY 18 OCTOBER 2014

Lesson 2: Always remember that organisations are all about culture, the culture of 'how and why things are done around here'. I talked to the staff about culture at every opportunity. I acknowledged that while it is the job of a senior team to set that culture, to explain and describe what it looks like in practice, to make expectations and standards crystal clear, it is equally the responsibility of every single member of staff to live up to those standards, to embody them, to model them constantly through words and actions. We developed a culture of aspiration and ambition for the students. Staff knew the high standards of professionalism that were expected of them, and they lived up to them – how they spoke to the children, how they dressed, their own attendance and time keeping (staff with 100 per cent attendance got a box of chocolates at the end of each term, a small but appreciated gesture, and the number of boxes we needed rose every year).

It was really important to me when we opened that we were seen as a new school with a different culture. Clearly, when you are in the same building with the same children and – at the beginning at least – all the same teachers, this is a challenge. But it was vital. For a long time – to my frustration – people would still say, 'Oh yes, you've changed your name, haven't you?' But this was not a rebrand; a rebrand can often be cosmetic, with a new uniform, name and logo merely some new icing on the same stale old cake. A rebrand can often just be a gear change, but we needed a whole new car. I needed to start a new school from the inside, not tinker around with what was already there.

MONDAY 20 OCTOBER 2014

Simon is old beyond his years. This is something people often say about youngsters, and is equally as often untrue, but in his case, it is entirely accurate. And sadly, this is because he has to do things that no eleven-year-old should have to do. Simon looks after his disabled dad, his mother having died when he was three, so that on top of school he has a whole host of tasks that range from shopping to cleaning to cooking. He is likeable, personable, sharp. He wants to do well more than any other child I have ever met, but he regularly, often quite spectacularly, fails to do so. I know we aren't meant to have favourite students, but we all do, and he is definitely one of mine. Today, however, as is so often the case, I have to switch on Stern Teacher Face as he is brought to me for having been naughty in a supply teacher's lesson. (I love the word 'naughty'. Kids have always been, and always will be, naughty. And so they should be. Naughty is not swearing at teachers, it is not posting vile abuse online about a child in your class, it is not sending a class of little children running around screaming in terror as you use the teacher's staple gun to run rampage in your classroom.[*] Naughty is being mischievous, it is being silly, it is taking advantage of a weak supply teacher by hiding their marker or making daft noises. Today's crime is the latter.) With Simon, I use the language that has the most impact (on most students, and certainly on most adults), the language of 'disappointment', of 'letting yourself down', of 'what will dad think?' (always feel a bit mean using that one, but it works and it's true). As ever, he looks even more serious than me, keeps his little back straight (he is tiny) and promises me (not for the first time and undoubtedly not for the last) that it will not happen again. We set (another) target of merits to reach that week and off he trots.

WEDNESDAY 22 OCTOBER 2014

I receive an email from Sharon Butler, my feisty Attendance Manager.

Just to advise you that I have taken a very unpleasant phone call from Mrs Potts regarding Kirk and his Daily Detention this afternoon. I placed him on the detention list as he was late today, having, he said, 'woken up late', and I sent the usual

---

[*] My own primary class, 1975, Gary Deakin; I will never forget the look on his face, and I am totally convinced he is now in jail serving a life sentence for murder.

message out, but at the end of the day she came storming in and ranted at me that she 'hadn't got no sodding text!' I started to tell her that problems with her phone provider were not my problem, but she just kept ranting why weren't we giving 24 hours' notice. I informed her that legally we do not need to give *any* notice and that this could all be resolved if Kirk got into school at the right time, at which point she told me to go and fuck myself.

THURSDAY 30 OCTOBER 2014

One of my strongest appointments from the start of the year is Jeff. Jeff is my age, highly experienced and one of the best teachers I have ever worked with. Previously an electronic engineer, he brings so much real-world experience to the classroom, where he teaches engineering and graphics, and has the warmest, strongest relationships with the children, without ever crossing the line of professional adult. The kids adore him, as do I. His classroom this morning buzzes with the quiet hum of serious endeavour, the children's heads bent over their soldering. Simon is particularly engaged, determined that dad's Christmas will be made by his gift of a wobbly hand challenge game. I imagine dad's hand already wobbles quite a bit and may not beat the alarm that beeps when you hit the side of the twisty trail, but I also imagine the pride that will glow on Simon's face when his dad unwraps it on Christmas morning, and I feel my eyes well up. Jeff is sitting next to him, guiding his little hand as he solders, gently encouraging him without taking over.

As he talks to him, I am reminded that the way we talk to our children becomes their own inner voice, and it pains me to think of how much shouting and abuse so many of our children hear at home. I think that, as much as the knowledge that we impart is vital, it is the pupil–teacher relationships that are of such importance and are what makes the job so special.

THURSDAY 6 NOVEMBER 2014

Lesson 3: Engage with parents. Although at times, especially initially, it seemed as if we were at war with the parents and carers of our children, I had to keep reminding myself that many, many families were fully supportive of the direction of travel of the school. It was really important to keep families well informed of developments in the school and, crucially, to explain changes and decisions; I realised very early on that you can never over-communicate. Schools often refer to 'hard-to-reach families', but often it can be schools that are hard to reach, especially with parents who themselves may have bad memories of their own experience of education. I encouraged staff to contact home when students did well, not just when there were concerns, and I made a habit of finishing every day with a positive email or call. But of course, you can never please everyone.

I email my lovely chair of governors:

Hi Brian, hope all well. Got a good one for you! You may recall that Mrs Potts was a parent who was due in for our governor meeting, and she didn't turn up? I met her two weeks ago to discuss the 'go fuck yourself' incident. She actually apologised to me about this, agreeing it was totally unacceptable, and I stressed that if it was to recur I would look at banning her from the site. She accepted this, but then last week unfortunately we did have another outburst, this from my receptionist:

'Mrs Potts came into Reception – it was clear from her body language that she was livid. She shouted at me to get Mr Jones down here. I explained that Mr Jones was not available, but she just became more abusive and angry. She said that she would not leave until Mr Jones came down to speak to her. I went up to find him and he was teaching but he said that he was happy to see her if she makes an appointment. But when I relayed this message to Mrs Potts she again became abusive and angry, shouting, 'If you don't go and fucking get him right now I will jump over that desk and smash your face in, you stupid bitch.'

So, Brian, I would like your support please to now ban her from our site – what do you think?

WEDNESDAY 12 NOVEMBER 2014

It would seem that the Lunsford Locals are getting angrier:

JH: I'm not saying the kids should have phones out in class and if they do i think u should have them taken off till the end of the day but no longer! If they try taking my Tracy's they won't know what's hit em!

PW: Yeah, they just don't care about us, what if something happens on the way home? I can't live without my phone. My mum said if they try to take my phone off me to shove it where the sun don't shine!

LR: My mate who knows a lot about the law said it's theft from a miner. We used to be smart at school with our fags and lighters, maybe we should give the kids some lessons on being crafty!

SW: She only cares about image not the kids results.

VM: Ooh, not sure about sending mine next year then! ok having rules but surely they should be looking at their grade results more??

DH: No disrespect to you lovely ladies out there but see what occurs when you give a woman a position of power? … Look at good old Maggie (the milk snatcher) thatcher … goes straight to their heads!

LR: At the end of the day it's a school in Lunsford. Kids will always break the rools.

MONDAY 24 NOVEMBER 2014

Receive a letter from Mrs Harris. Her daughter is bright and extremely feisty, constantly challenging the rules, repeatedly in detentions. Mum fluctuates between seemingly supporting us (she cannot control her daughter at home either) and then blaming us. It's a common pattern; today it appears she has had enough of trying to cooperate.

My daughter Lorenna will not be coming back to your school, I am going to find her a better school where the teachers know how to deal with there pupils and care about every child's personal needs. Your school is ridiculous with all the rules. You do know you are running a school and not a prison? Mrs Taylor, you've been really kind, helped Lorenna out and I wish you all the best, the rest of you can fuck right off!

FRIDAY 5 DECEMBER 2014

I remember going to a high-end restaurant where we had waited weeks for a reservation. It was celebrating its 30th anniversary and the food was as delicious and memorable as I'd hoped. As is my wont, I got chatting to the waiter. It was a busy Saturday night, but he made time for us and answered my questions about the dishes and the restaurant's history. Finally, I asked him how long he'd worked there. 'Thirty years,' he replied, 'I am the owner.' It was a memorable and valuable lesson: of the absolute necessity of keeping an eye on the detail, of never seeing any job as beneath you, and – crucially – of being in touch with the daily reality and experience of the most valuable asset: your staff.

I email Charles:

Hi, I just wanted to say that I really appreciate everything that you're doing. I love you being in our team and I always enjoy our heated debates! Thank you for taking on the extra class, too, all those extra lunch duties, the open mornings, supporting in Daily Detention. I feel very lucky that we have people like you of such high calibre. I just hope that you are enjoying it along the way too! Have a good weekend.

He replies:

> Thanks very much. I love it and really want to repay your faith in me by delivering record results in history! It's a privilege to be a part of such a major transformation. I've developed quite an affinity for the place! Certainly would not have foreseen enjoying coming to work so much even a year ago!

SATURDAY 10 JANUARY 2015

Sitting in my office in Saturday detention, alone, the pupils yet again having not turned up; I'm not quite sure what I did to be here. My mum sends me a link to a TED Talk called 'How to fix a broken school? Lead fearlessly, love hard.'

'Saw this and thought of you,' she emails. I watch it and it's brilliant. Brings tears to my eyes. The tough and sassy New York head Linda Cliatt-Wayman's attitude chimes resolutely with my own, her mantra of, 'So what? Now what?' No excuses. Tough love. Zero tolerance. High expectations. I wonder if Linda managed to get them to turn up to detention on a Saturday.

MONDAY 12 JANUARY 2015

The Locals have the answer:

MK: From what I can make out they only get a Saturday detention if they don't turn up for there after school detentions.

SW: I bet no 1 will turn up for the stupid Saturday detention.

OY: Dead right, mate, if they don't turn up for the stupid

detention when they are already there, they sure as hell ain't going to get out of bed on a Saturday! LOL

TUESDAY 20 JANUARY 2015

My VP and I finish an especially taxing day and end up in the local trendy cocktail bar, designed for twenty-somethings not knackered teachers, which is becoming as familiar to me as my own lounge. We even have 'usual seats', which seems worryingly OK. 'Large or small?' asks the barman, not even needing to ask the colour, and then adds, 'Silly question.' We laugh, nervously.

The biggest challenge by far in this role is not difficult children or aggressive parents; it is staff recruitment. The myth of the 'superhead' is just that; I often describe myself as the conductor of the orchestra. Our eventual success will ultimately be because of the wonderful team of teaching and support staff that I hired. My job is to attract great staff and then to develop them professionally and to value them relentlessly, to nourish and to nurture, to look after them and care for them. I have had to move on many underperforming staff in my time. (Although give me a struggling but on-message teacher any time over the competent but subversive, the teacher who doesn't buy into and believe in the values and vision of the head. They are far, far more corrosive and toxic than a struggling teacher who cares, wants to improve and believes that all children can.) My favourites have included the head of biology who gripped my desk as I told him I was letting him go (a lot of people have gripped my desk over the years) and who shouted that God would punish me. I told him calmly that I reckoned God was far angrier at him for leading a subject where only 11 per cent of the children had gained exam success.

Teachers change lives. Teachers inspire and encourage, instil a love of learning and a love of their specialist subject. A government campaign of twenty years ago had a very successful advert to encourage recruitment to the profession. A succession of celebrities appeared on the screen, from the arts, from business, from the media, from science, from sport, all saying a single name. At the end it simply stated, 'Everyone remembers a good teacher.' Everyone recalls the name of someone who taught them ten, twenty, thirty or maybe just two or three years ago, who inspired them, really saw them and recognised potential in them. Similarly, they will recall the teacher who put them off learning, who was a bully, who couldn't keep order, who didn't mark their books, who was sarcastic, maybe even violent, and equally, those teachers leave their mark for ever.

Working in schools is unique. It can consume you. I never forget that my staff all have lives outside of school, all have families, relationships, challenges, all have things going on that are of immense importance: a child starting school, illness in the family, divorce, death. For this reason, I constantly thank my staff for giving so much of themselves, thank them for every restless or sleepless night, every date or occasion they were late for, or distant at, their mind elsewhere. I care about the impact my staff have on the children in our care. I don't notice whose car is the last in the car park, but I notice who plays table tennis with the students at break, who sits and eats their lunch with them, who spends their break duty in the canteen chatting to them. I notice the member of staff who, on her last day before she went on maternity leave, was walking around the school in all her free lessons, having a quiet and encouraging word with some of the most difficult students who would miss her calm, steady support. Our position carries with it a huge responsibility; it is one I consider a privilege, and one I never forget.

THURSDAY 5 FEBRUARY 2015

Dawn was almost certainly a foetal alcohol syndrome baby, but speculating on that is not how I kick off my meeting with mum, who has no front teeth and who smells of Thunderbird. Dawn is simmering, about to boil over. I have seen her like this on countless occasions. She is bright, tragic, neglected, angry. Today's particular misdemeanour is recounted – unkind messages on social media – and she starts with the usual 'everyone else…' mantra.

'We are not here with everyone else, and everyone else's mum, Dawn, we are here with *you* and *your* mum. There are a lot of us who care about you: me, Mrs Cresswell, mum, you have Tony from Early Help (note to self – that name needs changing to 'Never Early Enough')… But we can only *help* you; you need to do it.'

She still glowers; she has heard this many times. I show mum the phone with the messages on it. 'I can't read that without my glasses,' she lies, but we are not here to humiliate her, which she has clearly done a good enough job of already over the years, judging by the evident contempt her daughter has for her. In any case, she won't allow her own poor literacy to hold her back, and she starts to lay into Dawn, aggressively, angrily, culminating (helpfully) in, 'You're going into a care home.'

Dawn is crying now while simultaneously shouting, 'I don't care.' Clearly her mother's late taking up of the parenting baton hurts her deeply, but all she can yell to her mum is, 'You're such a liar, be quiet.'

Mum sneers. 'I've been on the planet more than you, my thirty-seven to your twelve.'

To which Dawn retorts, 'Thirteen not twelve.'

'Just like your useless father, turn everything into an argument.' She turns to me. 'She needs a behaviour school.'

'No, she doesn't, she needs to behave,' I say.

'She needs something done with her,' she spits. 'She's got special needs. ADHD.'*

And I want to say, 'Yes, she certainly has needs. She needs another mum, she needs love and boundaries, she needs guidance and care. Affection and rules. Someone to talk to her and read with her, someone who turns up to parents' evening, and who hasn't spent their daughter's entire life snorting drugs and then expects their bright, hurting, lonely child to respect them.' But I just stand up, call the meeting to a close and mum

---

*   ADHD, or attention deficit hyperactivity disorder, is a mental health disorder that can cause above-normal levels of hyperactive behaviour and make it harder to pay attention. It has become the catch-all excuse of modern times in many dysfunctional families. Rather than become one of those cynics who claim it doesn't exist, I prefer to listen to science, to psychology, to research; it undoubtedly exists. But far too often in failing schools, where there is not good order in the classroom, or in failing families where routines, structure and good behaviour are not taught, it is common for parents to look to a set of initials to blame rather than to look in the mirror.

wanders back down the stairs, Dawn trailing after her, to go back to a home and an evening I don't want to think about.

MONDAY 23 FEBRUARY 2015

Simon runs up to me in the playground at breaktime, beaming. I ask him how it's going. 'I'm having a really great week, miss, brilliant, no demerits and no detentions!' I feel reluctant to point out to him that we're only two hours into the week.

Only those who have worked in a failing school truly understand what it is like. You can read about it, criticise it, imagine it and sympathise with teachers who are in it. But unless you have lived the reality, you don't get it, can't know how it feels to struggle in every day, to plan lessons that you can never teach, to set detentions for children who will never turn up, to feel the isolation and loneliness in a classroom that is never visited by a senior teacher and where the children smell your fear, and play on it.

I would not have been able to teach in Castlecliffe; it is a marvel that some did. These were the teachers with experience, who could close their doors and keep their classrooms as an oasis of (relative) calm, who in truth did not see the chaos and carnage of other teachers' lessons, nor the number of children roaming corridors or causing havoc at lunchtime. I saw it all. It used to break my heart, knowing that for a time, some of this would continue, that schools cannot be turned around overnight and that some teachers, despite the systems and rules we were establishing, and the expectations we were raising, would still suffer. I'd comfort myself with the knowledge that at least it would no longer be in silence.

When I first started in Castlecliffe, I asked the heads of year to give me the top five 'naughties' in their year group. It was clearly a challenge whittling it down to just five, as I ended up with thirty-nine names, every one of whom I met, with their families – usually mum, sometimes an older sibling. Rarely two parents. I told them what was going to be changing, what the new standards and expectations were going to be, what would happen if their child carried on behaving badly. Rather surprisingly, virtually every one of them supported me, said it was long overdue; most of them made a rueful comment about how teachers were no longer able to 'give him a wallop'. For most, their son (so often a son) was out of their control at home, too. I will never forget one parent, whose son was in Year 10, nodding along with everything I said, and then saying, simply, 'He won't last; he's got away with it here for too long.' She was right. He didn't.

WEDNESDAY 18 MARCH 2015

I am contacted by the local BBC TV team: they want to do a piece on our mobile phone ban. (We have had, since day one, a policy stating that mobile phones are not to be seen anywhere in school, and if they are, they are confiscated until the end of the term.) I think, as I so often do, that there can't be a lot of news about if 'school has high standards' is newsworthy, but I agree to do it, for the same reason I only ever do this sort of thing: to publicise the school's name and our high expectations. The interviewer persists on linking our phone ban to our improvements; I repeatedly point out that the phone issue is just one element of a much larger improvement strategy. She asks me if it's been successful; I relay how we rarely ever have to confiscate a phone now, and reference the start of the year when I had to deal with some parents who were 'rather irate' (bit of a euphemism, that). I use the line I have used 100 times: 'I have met plenty of parents who want their child to give them a quick call to say they got to school OK, or to text them if they are a bit late on the way home, but I've never met a parent yet who wants their child to be on Facebook in their French lesson or texting their mate in maths.' She asks me if the ban is here to stay – 'All the time I'm here, yes' – and I make my point about the irony of how things that were invented to improve communication are now, in my view, in danger of creating a generation of children with extremely poor communication skills.

TUESDAY 14 APRIL 2015

I have never had a PA, never wanted or needed one. I've always felt that, in a school, they can become a real obstacle and block between staff and leadership. However, there is so much non-classroom work that needs doing, and which distracts me, that I reluctantly concede that I need to appoint one. I am inundated. Over 175 applications. When I get home from school I sit with a (large) glass of wine, reading every single one. Most go in the bin – I need someone to help me, to have the same standards and attention to detail as I do, not send in an application with typos or misusing 'their'. Some also provide a laugh: 'I feel my punctuality is excellent. Whenever I'm going to be late I will always ring to let management know.'

'I have a great sense of humour. You bloody need one in this office.'

But about twenty end up in the 'possible' pile, clearly professional and committed women – they are all women – and one in particular stands out, or rather leaps out. Young, excellent academic record, eloquent, thoughtful. She is working as a manager at Primark; why is it that if it had been John Lewis it would appear more impressive? I shortlist her. I end up appointing her. For the next five years, Claire is my right-hand woman and I have never cared for a fellow colleague more.

FRIDAY 17 APRIL 2015

I see Dave, a PE teacher, in the corridor looking flustered. I ask him what's up. He tells me that Georgie, a particularly challenging and disaffected Year 11 student, isn't in again, so he'd rung home, to be told by mum that the reason is because 'she's had lip fillers again and 'er lips are all bruised'.

'So not just damaging her life chances but also her face by the sounds of it,' he says gloomily.

SUNDAY 19 APRIL 2015

Lesson 4: Get the curriculum right. Ensuring that the curriculum is broad, balanced and appropriate lies at the heart of a great school. We did a lot of work on the curriculum in all subjects, to ensure a joined-up and logical progression in learning, ensuring that children were learning in a sequential manner, building on prior knowledge and never repeating or duplicating work that had been taught before (other, obviously, than when extending a topic or revising). A great curriculum should be all about 'the best that has been thought and said', and we had a duty to ensure that our students were taught a knowledge-rich curriculum and that they attained the necessary background knowledge that would allow them to compete successfully with children from more affluent backgrounds. One of the best staff sessions we held early on was to get everyone to discuss 'Thirty things every young person should know when they leave school if we are to have truly delivered a great education'. The final list would have made anyone well versed in all thirty topics an excellent member of a pub quiz team, but it was fascinating to see how so many of the things that we considered important were not actually being taught – art history, early civilisation, famous composers, economics, political awareness, to name but a few – so we created opportunities to teach them. We extended the school day with an extra-curricular provision ranging from science club to debating to teddy bear making, we held termly Academy Days that allowed us to cover a particularly important subject or issue in real depth, and we held our own version of TED Talks to expand further our students' cultural capital.

MONDAY 1 JUNE 2015

Six months ago, Charles, my lovely Teach First history lead who I have seconded onto the leadership team at considerable expense (but who is too good to risk losing), came to see me, very excited. It turns out his best friend's mum is a national newspaper editor (Charles is not just a great teacher, he moves in great circles apparently). So interested is his friend's mum in the stories Charles tells when he is round at their house for dinner, in the challenges we face and how we are improving the school (and of course the abuse we are getting from some families), that she thinks it would make a great features article. Will I meet a journalist his friend's mum has recommended, Charles asks? He knows it's risky, he knows that in general we don't trust journalists, he knows it could all backfire, but he thinks it's a great opportunity to publicise the positives and counter the negative media we have experienced. I know what the CEO of the trust will say. I know what the rest of the leadership team will say. I know what my partner will say. But I say, 'Absolutely, thanks, what a great opportunity.'

Fast-forward to today. I have just shown the journalist around. He seems lovely. He seems genuine. He talks about his own childhood as a fostered child and how much he respects the work that people like us do in schools and communities like these. I sit with him and am as candid, blunt and open as I always am. I know it is a huge gamble. I know I risk exposing the school to the harsh light of publicity and he may be a smiling assassin, he may want a sensational article and to focus on the things we haven't yet completed, the areas where there is still much to do rather than on the shining successes of bringing calm and order where previously there was chaos and mess and failure.

I am sitting in a large room, trying to blend into the background, as he interviews a range of pupils. I am there as a safeguarding presence but not to talk or censor. I am tapping away

41

at my computer, feigning deafness, but after a while I just sit and listen, concentrating on suppressing the smile that wants to spread over my face as I listen to the children's innocent, accurate capture of what was wrong with the old school.

'We used to have counselling, but it didn't work at all, don't think he was even a proper counsellor, think he just wanted some easy cash, he used to just sit there on his phone.'

'The old school apparently was a sports college, but we didn't even do much sport. Just played football. Sometimes.'

'Mr Jones gets a lot of abuse online from some parents, but he's one of the best teachers in the school, he doesn't sit down once in lessons, he's mad about maths. He's strict because he doesn't want us to be like the students in the old school who fail and then are crying at the end of the year when they get their results.'

And my favourite, said with a look of genuine puzzlement by a pupil who was a nightmare in the old school and is really turning it around, 'I just don't understand how they got away with it for so many years?'

The journalist ends by asking them what one thing they would change. I sit silently listing at least twenty areas where we still have much to do. A little voice pipes up: 'I don't think there is much to change.'

TUESDAY 2 JUNE 2015

Ironically, as someone who has often chosen to work in so-called challenging schools where behaviour is poor, I have never liked the idea of having to be good at 'behaviour management'; teachers shouldn't have to be. Teachers should be experts in their field, inspiring, well qualified, enthusiastic, optimistic, kind, professional, and want to build strong, positive relationships with their young charges. This was the first priority in our school.

I also don't actually like the overused term 'zero tolerance', which sounds so dramatic and harsh and unpleasant, when in fact it means high standards, aiming for the best. I always think: nobody ever aims for a third-class degree so why would anyone aim for, or accept, mediocrity? Ours was definitely a tough kind of love. Children are children and there will always be behaviour issues; children make mistakes, for one thing (just like us adults, except that they have no life experience to draw upon). But in the disadvantaged and spiritually impoverished community we were in, there were some extreme behavioural concerns. In my experience, such extreme behaviour usually came from one of three sources. There are those parents who spoil and over-indulge their children, who give in to everything, give them whatever they want (including not going to school), never see anything wrong in them but find fault in everything the school does. Then there are the homes where there is no parenting; those sad, truly tragic, chaotic homes, where dysfunctionality is the norm, where children are unkempt and uncared for, unloved and unnurtured, Broken Britain at its saddest and most damaging. And finally (and this has seen the largest increase in my time in education) those parents for whom there is an excuse for anything their child does wrong and which usually involves a number of initials,

ADHD being the most common, although any collection of SEND* acronyms will do, and usually the more the merrier.

We had lots of all three.

• • •

Martina is confused (and confuses me). At heart she is a nice girl, with a very nice mum. She is bright and opinionated (which I like) but too often stroppy and rude (which, obviously, I don't). She wants to play the bad girl, but she isn't one. She can cause a lot of disruption to lessons and I spend a good deal of time thinking about how best we can get her back on track. She isn't unloved, isn't neglected (not obviously so) and wants to do well (although I believe this of every child, to be honest, even the ones who don't know it themselves). I spend hours talking to Martina about her life, her future, how her poor behaviour is whittling away at this, and at her chances of ever becoming the architect she wants to be. Today mum is in for yet another meeting. I am at a bit of a loss as to what to do. I tell

---

* SEND is a legal definition. It stands for special educational needs and disabilities. A child is best defined as having these needs if they have a learning problem or disability that makes it more difficult for them to learn than most children their age. In England it is estimated that 1.3 million children have SEND and many do not make the progress that children of their age should. Too often, failing schools think a child with a learning need cannot make progress and they will write them off (if not openly), lower their expectations, provide easy work, give them the worst teachers, when in reality they need and deserve the very best. In addition, the system to get properly funded support in schools is ridiculously bureaucratic and complicated. Add to that another layer of many parents labelling their own children with a SEND when the facts are yet again poor parenting and low expectations, and it is not surprising, though it is depressing, that so many of the most vulnerable youngsters in education yet again are not adequately served.

mum I can exclude Martina (easily), but it doesn't seem to have much impact, that we can't keep carrying on like this, that she is using up her lives and we need to see a turnaround. Soon. Martina is on her usual winning form, making all the right assurances. Mum is angry. 'You've got to sort this out, I'm fed up with this. You know how to behave. You'll end up like Mike and Laura next door at this rate.' This said with raised eyebrows and a frown of such ferocity that I can only deduce that ending up like Mike-and-Laura-next-door is not something anyone should aspire to. I don't imagine either is an architect.

WEDNESDAY 3 JUNE 2015

Last week I sent a thank-you card to a young teacher who started in Castlecliffe and is struggling with some challenging classes but has from day one been hugely encouraging and shown tremendous warmth to me. This morning I walk in to find a handwritten letter on my desk:

Every once in a while, a person does something special for you and it changes your mindset entirely. That is what happened when I read your card on Friday morning. I have been feeling rock bottom lately and knowing that the support that I have given *you* is so appreciated, well, it has lifted my spirits completely. Thank you for all the belief *you* have in me. I now have my strength and courage back, and being a teacher has always been my dream. Alice.

What a privilege this job is.

MONDAY 8 JUNE 2015

I'm approached at breaktime by a clearly rattled maths teacher. He has had a small catch-up group of disaffected Year 11s with him all morning, on intense revision for the forthcoming exams.

'How have they been?' I ask him cheerily.

'Unfocused and barely working. They really seem to have a "don't care" attitude to it all. The first line of the morning was from Jake who told me, "I'm not feeling up to this, sir. I've been on a three-day bender, and I'm only here to avoid a fine."'

TUESDAY 9 JUNE 2015

Cheryl's dad is in again, for yet another meeting about his daughter's prolonged periods of unauthorised absence. (He faces yet another fine from the local authority, although there being so many fines issued the courts can never, in reality, collect them nor take action against those who just choose not to pay.) Although this is not a child who is known for upholding the highest standards of uniform, the claim this time is that Cheryl hasn't got shoes and dad can't afford to get them yet.

'And you know what she's like, she won't wear thirty quid shoes, you know what I mean?' he tuts, nudging Cheryl, who sits bouncing her leg truculently next to him.

Actually, no, I don't, I say, I would have thought thirty quid shoes were ideal, seeing as how kids grow out of them so quickly, and in any case as her father *you* should be telling *her* what she will and won't do.

Cheryl is muttering angrily under her breath.

I give dad a death-stare and he drawls, 'She is in your school and her behaviour is your responsibility.'

I reply very slowly and deliberately, 'No, Mr O'Neill, when she is in my school, my responsibility is her progress, her learning and her safety – but her behaviour is *always* your responsibility, as her parent.'

Cheryl starts screaming at me, accusing me of being rude to her dad. 'My behaviour is *your* responsibility!' she shouts at me, to which I again reply, now directly to her, that how she behaves is, in fact, as much her responsibility as her dad's, at which point she tells me she doesn't 'give two fucks'.

I look directly at dad. 'Mr O'Neill, is this OK?'

'Cher, shut the fuck up,' he barks, and slams out of my office.

I am reminded of a meeting I had last week with a parent of an especially difficult Year 9 boy. I had read an article by a leading head teacher who spoke about how, when she meets with parents of disruptive pupils, she tells them they are bad parents. If their child won't go to school, won't follow the rules, won't behave and won't be polite, then they are bad parents because part of a good parent's responsibility is to teach their children from an early age to do all these things. Don't say they are bad people, she warns, but tell them they are bad parents because they are not taking this responsibility properly. Perhaps I didn't read the detail carefully enough, because it's fair to say that my first attempt at this approach, during my meeting with said Year 9 boy's father, is spectacularly unsuccessful, the shouts of abuse and swearing being heard all along the corridor, such that staff come up to me for the rest of the day to ask me if I am all right.

MONDAY 15 JUNE 2015

Lesson 5: The people in any organisation are its greatest asset and must be valued, constantly. Improving schools ultimately comes down to strong leadership, but equally as important as holding people to account and not accepting mediocrity is caring for and appreciating great staff. It is important as it is the right thing morally to do, but it is also, obviously, hugely important in a profession where recruitment and retention are such a challenge. We would look for opportunities to praise and acknowledge hard work and great teaching, and leaders would regularly write a quick appreciative email or card. We invited the whole cleaning team to coffee and mince pies at Christmas and remembered people's birthdays. We looked at ways to improve work–life balance, and since so often meetings and much paperwork in schools are pointless, we rarely did either. In the staff survey, twice a year, I asked if there was anything we did in school that staff felt was unnecessary or irrelevant; it was so important to keep taking a temperature check of the reality of being a teacher and to stay connected with the chalkface.

• • •

I remember Bethan, a young Australian supply teacher, well. In the first few weeks of my time at Castlecliffe, where I spent the vast majority of my time during the day in lessons, simply observing, she was trying valiantly to teach German. Every lesson was a disaster, the children just turning up to mess around, to mock, to jeer and to reduce her to tears on a daily (hourly) basis. She came to see me about a discussion she'd had, a few weeks before my arrival, with the (now former) VP who was supposed to be supporting her and who had given her brutal feedback on the lesson he had observed.

'At the end of the feedback I asked, "Was there anything in my lesson that went well?"' she explained to me. 'But his response was – "No, nothing."

'When I mentioned how I try to explain to students the importance of learning and knowing a second language, how it can help with employment, how you're exposed to new cultures – lots of positive things to try to get them to enjoy German – I was told to "cut the crap, just tell them it's on their timetable so they need to be there, that's it".'

She went on to tell me about the German club she had started at lunchtime, the handful of students who came to her after school for support and advice about their education. I was so sad; here was a young teacher, dedicated, intelligent, hard-working, committed – and receiving scant support and mentoring from those who, leaving aside their moral duty, were being paid to do so. I spent hours with her, including sitting making numerous phone calls to parents, modelling how to get parents on her side, how to try to re-establish herself after things had gone so spectacularly badly. I observed her lessons and gave constructive, honest feedback.

A couple of months after I started mentoring her, she emailed me:

I know I need to stop thanking you, but I can honestly say my time here has changed so much. I feel more confident in my lessons and I am really enjoying coming to work, knowing I have you to support me. Before, I felt lost, and that matters would never improve. My family knew I was having a tough time here and all of them are now so happy that my career seems to have turned a corner. I can't thank you enough for all of your help. I can feel how you are making a difference and helping this school move forward.

I replied:

I really enjoy working with you, and I know that together we will make a real impact on those students causing trouble. It takes time, but like I said, our purposeful practice pays off! Let's just carry on seeing students together, speaking to parents, giving detentions, giving praise, seeing students doing well in other places around school, and I know you are going to go from strength to strength. You have the makings of a really great teacher and I am going to help you to become one. Please don't thank me – I want to thank *you* for all the effort and hard work you are putting in, when it must be difficult such a long way from home. Never forget – we are a team and you are not on your own in anything! Nothing is ever too small to talk to me about. Teaching is a great job!

MONDAY 22 JUNE 2015

Ricky doesn't take much work. Doesn't need the hotshot

interrogator. Doesn't require me to play good cop/bad cop with my pastoral team. 'Yeah, I did it,' he shrugs. He leans against the wall, not so much insolent and angry as resigned and apathetic. The 'it' in question today was setting off the fire alarm, a major misdemeanour in itself – I have calculated that to evacuate the school like this costs in excess of £2,000 in teacher hours and represents countless hours of lost learning. It always ends in an exclusion. The kids know this. To be honest, they get as annoyed as the teachers to be dragged from their classes (unless it is a lesson they don't much like) and on top of this today it is tipping it down.

I try the be-calm-in-order-to-scare approach. 'Ricky, I don't understand why you do it, you know we have cameras, you know we exclude, you know you're in trouble, I am really disappointed and on top of that we are all drenched – including you.' Another shrug. 'The obvious question is why?' But I know I am only going to get another shrug.

I really like Ricky, one of those 'likeable rogues' of olden times. I know that in a few years if I come across him in the street with a group of his mates he will greet me with friendly chirpiness rather than mug me. In addition, I really like his mum. I sigh and say, 'Mum will go mad.' It is a statement of fact that only gets another shrug, but I know that he cares really. This is one child I am never giving up on. But I exclude him, of course, for five days.

SUNDAY 28 JUNE 2015

Although Sundays are meant to be downtime, I usually spend

most of them either thinking about school or reading about education. I read a fascinating book on organisational culture: Stephen Covey, *The 7 Habits of Highly Effective People*. It suggests that only one in five employees see a correlation between their tasks and their organisation's goals, and only 37 per cent have a clear understanding of what their organisation is trying to achieve. I am absolutely determined that this will not be the case for our school, and I'm totally committed to creating that line of sight between what every one of my wonderful staff does and what we are striving to become. Everything that every one of them does is part of our bigger picture and will help us to realise our vision. In next morning's staff briefing, I tell my favourite story, of an unannounced visit by John F. Kennedy to the Space Center at Cape Canaveral in 1963. Kennedy toured the complex and met a man in overalls. 'What do you do here?' he asked. The man replied, 'I'm earning a living.' Kennedy nodded and moved on. He met another man in overalls and asked him the same question. 'I clean away all the rubbish,' the man said. Kennedy smiled and strode on until he met another man in overalls and put the same question again. This time a big smile came across the face of the man, who replied, 'Mr President, I'm helping to put a man on the moon.'

THURSDAY 9 JULY 2015

Lesson 6: Set (and keep) your expectations sky high. From day one we had the highest of expectations for our students (and staff) and while many frequently fell short it did not mean we lowered what we expected from them. We had high expectations of how the children should behave, of how they moved around the building, of how they came into assembly. We had high expectations of how they presented their work and would make students rewrite anything that fell short. We had high expectations of attendance; my pastoral team frequently turned up at the homes and indeed bedrooms of children with poor attendance and on several occasions marched them out of bed and back into school. (I had one head teacher friend who also removed the TV from the child's bedroom and told the parent they could collect it at the end of term!) We had high expectations of where they would go when they finished school; we spoke constantly about university, explaining what it was and why they should aim for going, and we held conferences where successful women and men from the community came in and spoke about their careers. We understood the challenges many of our young people experienced and were sympathetic to this but without ever allowing excuses or lowered expectations to creep in. Our strict uniform rules represented these high expectations and we enforced them constantly, for even the smallest of transgressions, to maintain consistent standards.

The Wellbeing Manager grabs me on the corridor, 'I'd sent Cheryl to Isolation* for being in trainers, but then I saw her

---

* The most severe sanction any school has is to exclude children from school, a legal action but one that, of course, often leaves children just hanging around the streets. Over the years many parents challenged me that it was not a punishment for their child to just sit at home playing computer games, to which I would wearily point out that no, indeed, having been punished by the school it would be very helpful if the parent supported that sanction by not letting their child sit at home and play computer games. We tried as often as possible not to exclude but rather to keep children out of lessons, and social circulation, working quietly all day in a supervised Isolation room.

trying to sneak into her first lesson, still in trainers. I stepped in front of her, but she just argued repeatedly, refusing to change into school shoes (which I could see were in her bag). She kept saying I was unfair, as it wasn't her fault, she wasn't feeling well, her shoes are too tight etc. But then she just walked away and left school. FYI, I have called her dad but when I told him that she'd walked away, he said, "Don't blame her! I've told her not to take any crap from you lot and just to walk away when someone's taking the piss.'"

FRIDAY 10 JULY 2015

David sends me a prank email:

> It is with great regret that I have to announce that I am to leave The Lunsford Academy. Its all that bloody principles fault. She's a bleeding nightmare to work with. Since she got her photo in the paper she thinks shes the bloody primes minister. Lets hope the Locals get her and get her soon!!

'Hilarious,' I reply.

WEDNESDAY 22 JULY 2015

The end-of-term rewards assembly is a highlight of the school year. As I stand and watch them collecting their rewards and certificates, their faces a touching mixture of stifled pride, teenage embarrassment and childish joy, I am yet again frustrated at the number of faces whose names I don't know, whose success I have been unaware of, children with difficult lives or easy ones, one parent, two, none, but who every day come in, work hard, try their best, are kind and sensible. I know a number of the children in this room inside out, their chaotic lives, their dysfunctional families, their behaviour records like the back of my hand. Yet again I vow that next term I will learn every pupil's name, will spend time with all of them, and less time with the hard core who occupy so much of my day and so much of my head. I am not confident I will succeed.

POSTSCRIPT

I am in Rome. The article about the school is live and has run on the newspaper's website this morning. I know there will be photos of the children, of us. I have no idea what the article will say, and if my trust will backfire, or if I will look fat (this, I know, is not important). It is summer but there is an unexpected thunderstorm in Rome, and we are sheltering in the train station, watching rain fall in torrents and lightning crack against the Roman sky. My brother texts me a smiley face. I am desperately trying to download the article on my phone. There is no Wi-Fi. I am literally shaking. Have I exposed my staff and pupils to further negative publicity, further ridicule? Will I be sacked from a job I love and where there is so much more to do?

Finally, I manage to get it downloaded and as I read the text on my tiny phone, tears stream down my face. It is accurate, honest and frank. It reflects exactly what we are doing and why. It is open, warm and touching. The journalist has captured not only the struggles we face, but the blood, sweat and tears we are all putting into making things better, and, most importantly, our motive – not money or fame but to transform children's life chances.

I don't know as I read it that we are going to be again inundated with emails of support from people all round the UK. I don't know that I am going to get handwritten letters from people I have never met, nor ever will, saying things like, 'It's a sad state of affairs when parents can't simply abide by common-sense rules.' I don't know that a man will sit down and write me an email: 'I just had to write to you after reading the article this morning. Teaching is such an important job but it seems to me at times it is an impossible one. Can I pass on my heartfelt and sincere congratulations to you and your team on what was a very inspiring read over my coffee this morning. Britain needs more teachers like you!' I don't yet know that a man I will know only as P. Raynor will send me a cheque for £4,000, with 'no strings', which we use to fund a school trip to London. I don't know as I read that Nick Gibb, recently appointed Minister for School Standards at the Department for Education, is also reading it and I will get a phone call from his people saying, 'The Minister was really inspired to read the recent article about your school. He has asked if you would find an hour to come and meet him in the Department?' One of the areas in his remit, I later find out, is behaviour, so it appears 'he'd be especially interested in what has gone on in your school'. I don't know yet that when I do meet him, I will sit there surrounded by civil servants and red boxes and get the chance to talk directly to a minister of state about how schools need to be improved and how we need more teachers coming into the profession.

All I know is that I am proud and relieved and I am crying.

CHAPTER 2

2015–2016

'*The best way out is always through.*'

– ROBERT FROST

MONDAY 3 AUGUST 2015

I am on holiday in Italy. It is pouring. Locals tell me (repeatedly, thanks) that it hasn't rained like this for fifty years. Receive a cheering email from a friend who has read our article:

Hey, loved the article – and just as well, I invested three quid of my own money buying an online subscription It was great stuff. As you know, me being a miserable old git, not a lot impresses me these days, but you've really pulled it off. Good on you, girl! You deserve all the credit for the changes achieved at the academy. Sorry to hear about Rome being a washout, assume the bars are dry though. And if you fancy having a go at being a politician, well, I'd vote for you. B

I also start to receive emails from parents:

> Thank you for letting our little Frank do the interview with the journalist. Frank loves school, and we are so happy with how well he has settled. All his teachers have been amazing and helped him adjust to what has been a significant change, coming from a tiny village school, with only seven other children in his class. It is so lovely for me to see him so happy and enthusiastic when I drop him in the mornings, and then when he comes out with a wide grin, bubbling with excitement to tell me about his day. As parents, we have been impressed in all our dealings with staff at the school and their commitment to the academic success of the students. It is so wonderful to find teachers who view their profession as a vocation, not just a job.

TUESDAY 4 AUGUST 2015

The constant rain lends itself to doing very little; I email my thanks to the journalist who wrote our piece. He replies instantly:

> I am pleased, and relieved! The school has been on my mind since the article was published. It's fantastic that you've had an encouraging response. Every so often in my job a piece comes along which opens your eyes to other people's lives and sticks with you – the article about your school was one such piece. If it's helped to raise your profile and that of the children, then I'm delighted. Do let me know if you'd like me to come in to talk to the students about journalism and/

or give them some help with setting up a newspaper. Best of luck on results day. Let me know how the children get on.

I reread one of the lovely emails I am getting:

I read with great interest the article about your school this morning and I felt compelled to write to you. I am a parent at a small rural primary school which had a change of head last year. She has put in many positive changes but the reaction among some of the parents and staff alike has been terrible, with seven out of the twelve staff leaving and nineteen pupils out of eighty being removed by their parents. The situation at your school has so many similarities with what happened at our little school — too much pandering to people and not enough strong leadership by the former head. Disciplined and focused pupils will ultimately be best prepared for the challenges of life ahead of them.

I reply with brief thanks – it's still pouring – and get a reply almost immediately (maybe it is raining there too):

I am glad that you found my words encouraging! Our new head, like you, has had to withstand unpleasant and even occasionally abusive language from parents — which I think is unbelievable. I never understand parents who fight back against authority or think that rules make their little darlings unhappy. I am sure that the children at Lunsford are so much happier now than they were when the school was so unruly.

WEDNESDAY 26 AUGUST 2015

The academy's first set of exam results are in: the first for the school and, of course, the first for me. The headline is just 32 per cent of pupils getting five or more GCSEs at C or above, including English and maths.* It is of course an increase of over 10 per cent across the year group, and in fact if we didn't have to include in the figures the thirteen pupils who I have never even seen, as they either stopped coming to the school years before or had gone to a referral unit (but who we are still, theoretically, accountable for), it would be 41 per cent, and above the current floor target. It is a start, and behind those figures are some huge gains – science up by 25 per cent, English up by 35 per cent; 76 per cent of the pupils passing in history, 92 per cent in statistics. But, of course, it is nowhere near good enough and will still put us as the lowest-performing non-selective school in the area. The Lunsford Locals will love it. I won't be explaining to them that a failing school is like a huge oil tanker: you cannot turn it around instantly; that the children have only had one year of improved teaching (with some teaching still woefully inadequate and some subjects still not fully staffed) and that if you have had four years of dreadful

---

* Schools and education are about so much more than exam results and grades, and yet it is on those that the press and countless commentators fixate (although where potential is not reached and students are allowed to underperform that is, of course, an outrage). GCSE stands for General Certificate of Secondary Education and was introduced in 1988 to establish one national qualification, replacing the old CSEs and the more academically challenging O levels. Ranging from A to G, with a C generally regarded as a pass, in 1994 a new A* grade was also introduced. The measure of success, of five GCSEs at C or above, was later changed to include English and maths, to prevent schools from gaming the system by allowing pupils to sit softer, easier subjects. In 2017, just as most people finally understood A to G, they changed the grading system to 1 to 9, with 9 being highest. Maybe the government just likes people to be confused.

maths teaching, one year of good teaching cannot make up for the four years when nothing was learnt; that there is more to school than exam results and we already have a culture and ethos that is unrecognisable from what was previously the norm; that I receive emails on a daily basis supporting what we are doing and applauding our high standards and no-nonsense approach; that recruitment is getting slightly better. That will sound too much like excuses, and we don't do excuses. Ever.

THURSDAY 27 AUGUST 2015

I'm visiting my dad. We have never had the best of relationships; I suspect we are too alike, both fiery, both outspoken, both intolerant of mediocrity. In recent years we have reached something of a rapprochement, not least I suspect because he is now suffering from stage 4 lung cancer. Dad smoked seventy a day from the age of sixteen, gave up forty years later and has never touched one since. However, twenty-two years on, it sadly appears, they have caught up with him. He is remarkably cheerful, though, and we talk about the recent exam results. He has always been very interested in politics and education, something else no doubt I have inherited from him. I tell him they've increased but not enough, nowhere near enough, and I talk about oil tankers. He is incredulous when I tell him that we will be judged on the results of the thirteen children who I have never met. 'So, you're telling me that you are held to account for the results of children you've never met, who have not been taught by your teachers, who haven't even set foot in the building at any point in the last three years?' I nod. 'Bloody ridiculous.'

TUESDAY 1 SEPTEMBER 2015

I have to get the tone right in my speech to staff: I have to inspire and motivate, encourage and enthuse, but without overdoing it – the results need to get much better – and leaving nobody in any doubt that there is much, much still to do. But as I'm speaking, I think of what we all achieved last year, the numerous successes. I think of the excellent support for our trainee teachers (the hours of coaching, of mentoring, of supportive feedback, of mopping up tears), of increased attendance at parents' evenings and the positive parent surveys ('my child is well looked after at this academy – 92 per cent agreement'). I think of all the initiatives, events, processes that didn't exist in Castlecliffe but are now a firmly established and much loved part of Lunsford, such as the students who did their maths and English exams early and got great grades, of the prefects, and the memorable assemblies. I reflect on the success of our new reading room, and the joy of seeing older students help younger ones to read. I think of the spelling bee, of our maths competition, the cross-country (well, round the town) championships, all the charity days, of the gradually improving behaviour, better uniform, student pride, clear rules, high expectations, a school trip to Paris, a trip to the Tower of London, sports day, art and textiles creations, technology work. Our critics don't seem to see any of this, and certainly don't hear me talk constantly about how important *enjoyment* of school is; how, for me, enjoying school is *equally* as important as academic success.

I think I get the tone right – everyone looks sombre and intent, although to be honest on the first day back after six weeks it's not often people look happy.

Later I receive an email from Olivia. She is a wonderful English teacher in her second year.

I thought your words about the vision were fantastic; a very moving and powerful clarion call! I almost stood up to whoop and clap. Staff need to hear exactly what you said, and I think the students should hear a similar version. Every person I spoke to afterwards was captivated by it, so powerful. Can I please have a copy of your speech?

Think I hit the right note then.

FRIDAY 11 SEPTEMBER 2015

Gavin is one of those children who, whenever I see him, I smile. I don't really know why; he can be a little terror. He has a double-barrelled surname, not through any middle-class pretensions but because in this area both last names command the same degree of respect as each other. Clearly when Gavin and his sister Maria came along, mum and dad were both equally keen to keep their respective family names alive and kicking. Unfortunately, mum also liked to keep her spice addiction alive and kicking, a habit she picked up during one of her frequent stays at HMP, and ever since the children have been with us, it is dad we deal with, or nan. I don't know why but, to this day, knowing a child doesn't have a stable mum around makes my heart ache for them more than if they don't have a dad. It is irrational and unfair (and perhaps part of the reason is because there are scores of children in this school, and thousands more around the country, who don't know who their fathers are, let alone have any contact with them). But it does. It doesn't allow me to give them any more let-up. But it makes me think that little bit more about them on the way home.

Gavin is not, however, having the best half-term. The Vice-Principal already had to haul him out on the first day, and this is now week two. But I already love him. Keen, sparky, loveable, like a 21st-century Lunsford version of the Artful Dodger. He's on the corridor, lessons have begun.

'Why aren't you in class, Gavin?'

'I'm lost, miss. And I'll now probably be in even more trouble.' This is said with very sincere-seeming gloominess.

'Not if you're lost, Gavin. It's a genuine mistake, isn't it? You weren't trying to be lost, were you? You are trying to find the room, aren't you?'

'Probably.'

'Probably or definitely, Gavin?'

MONDAY 14 SEPTEMBER 2015

Receive a cheery email from VP David:

> Hi boss, this probably needs one of our standard Staff Abuse letters. I have just listened to the answerphone message received this morning: 'This is Reg Miles, Marcia Miles's dad. Yes, she is off school today, we told you four weeks ago that

she would be off for her brother's wedding. If you have a problem with this then shove it up your arse, you really are taking the fucking piss.'

THURSDAY 1 OCTOBER 2015

Lesson 7: Embed excellent behaviour. This is only one aspect of failing schools, the one that always gets the most attention and the most press, but unless classrooms are calm and orderly there can never be good learning. We established strong and firm boundaries, something all children crave even if they don't know it. We had clear rules that we enforced in tiny detail; I would often say to parents who asked us about our 'strict approach' that actually, all we were doing was enforcing the rules – if a rule is no good or not needed, scrap it, but if it is necessary, use it! It isn't complicated, but it is astonishing how many schools have rules they simply don't enforce. We preached constantly the need for consistency, and I spoke on an almost daily basis about the importance of 'rowing together'. There was no one person identified as 'leading on behaviour', but rather everyone knew their responsibility and their role, every adult in the building, the canteen and site staff as much as the teachers. I repeated endlessly my mantra, 'You get what you accept', and told staff to accept nothing less from the children than the highest of standards. But despite our reputation for zero tolerance, and the criticism from several quarters for our approach, what was always frustrating was the lack of understanding from our critics that in fact our approach was 'warm-strict', underpinning all our rule enforcement and sanctions with warm, respectful relationships with the children in our care. Tough love in action.

Email from a prospective parent:

I feel I must thank you. I had huge doubts before coming to see your school last night. I moved here a year ago and I don't know the area. My friend's daughter came across to your academy from Woodfield School and she was worryingly behind; my friend is very positive about your school so I came to see it for my son. A young man called Steven showed us around and was a credit to the school. All the teachers we met were so friendly and professional, and I bet all they really wanted was to go home after a twelve-hour day, but they were all lovely. Your young maths woman is incredible! I have heard loads of horror stories about the old school and I must say you must like a challenge. There's loads of failing schools where I think you should take over and inject your high expectations. Anyway, too many people are always so quick to complain but slow to speak up when credit is due, so I wanted to email you. Keep up the good work!

FRIDAY 2 OCTOBER 2015

Even when a child is truly, spectacularly awful, rude beyond belief, aggressive, operating entirely out of the school's (and, needless to say, the parents') control, there is always a part of me that just feels sad. Even when you're being sworn at, spat at, jeered or riled, even when the child is undermining everything you are pouring your heart and soul into (and the hearts and souls of all those staff who work for you and to whom you have a deep duty of care), even as they stand and shout and threaten to burn the place down (several instances), I feel genuinely sorrowful that they are so damaged, so angry and have been so badly parented – indeed, have not *been* parented – that their start in life is seriously, possible terminally, poisoned.

Lucas started with us last year when he came into Year 7. Huge brown eyes, a little tubby, chestnut hair, the proverbial butter-wouldn't-melt looks. He struggled with reading and has made startlingly poor progress in the past twelve months, but he never did much to draw attention to himself. Then, at the start of this year, there was a monumental shift. It would have been easy to think he had been swapped, had not the same angelic appearance been kept, albeit with a new, demonic personality. Undoubtedly something significant had happened at home, but we had no evidence and a social services so snowed under with cases that our suspicions wouldn't even merit a phone call back. This was not the so-called 'low-level behaviour' (a term I would never accept in any case, as how can poor behaviour that disrupts children's learning ever be described as 'low-level'?), but rather numerous removals from class, calling teachers 'cunts', culminating in an exclusion. Interestingly, however, he doesn't seem to want to be excluded: although today he should be at home, he has somehow got into the school and is running through the corridors. Clearly home is no haven.

David and I manage to pincer him between Science 5 and the chemicals cupboard. After calm and gentle reason (which is met with a succession of 'fuck off, you cunts, you can't tell me what to do'), I decide to prove him wrong rather than argue him down, and so myself and David take a firm hold on each arm and half-drag, half-carry him to the lift. Every inch of the way he is flailing, he is swearing, he is attempting to bite us. At one point he wrestles his arm from my grip and tries to swing at me, David (somehow) managing to stop his clenched fist in its path, which would undoubtedly have made a pretty memorable imprint on my face. The torrent of abuse is incessant. When we finally get him to reception, mum is waiting, having been urgently summoned, but her presence makes no difference. The abuse continues and as we watch her walk off with him I feel nothing but sadness.

TUESDAY 13 OCTOBER 2015

The LLs are discussing our rules:

CC: If the rules state no gum then no gum. In our day if we brought the schools name to shame outside of school while in school uniform we would be for it. These kids should respect the rules, not get all arsey when they are caught breaking them.

RV: I got caught going up the down stairs when I was at school, so I got an hours after school detention. My mum stood by the rules, I was pissed off but I tell you I never did it again!

SW: She likes being in the paper, the woman is a power freak, be better off running the prison service.

JJ: I think I must be a lucky parent, I have never had any issue with this school, they've really helped bring my boy out of himself, his grades are all As and he works really hard now.

SW: That's my point, they only care about helping 'A' students.

JJ: Nah, he wasn't to start with, he was a right little shit to be honest, wasn't at all interested in school, I had lots of hassle with him but with the school support he's doing great now! x

WEDNESDAY 14 OCTOBER 2015

Gavin runs up to me in the corridor. He is brandishing a ten-pound note. 'Miss, I just found this in the playground, somebody must have dropped it, and they won't be able to get any lunch.' He slaps it in my hand and saunters off. I love our kids.

FRIDAY 16 OCTOBER 2015

My friends, in an attempt (I think) to be kind, have encouraged me to join an internet dating site. To be honest, going out is the last thing I feel like, but I have finally committed to a date, although I am more terrified by the prospect of this than any difficult encounter with an angry parent or challenging child. However, the initial encounter is encouraging. Looks like his photo, friendly eyes, asks me questions. Have you had many dates, I ask, and he happily tells me I am the fifth of the week, he has had one on consecutive days (not a teacher, obviously, going out on a school night), with another seven ahead. I am exhausted by the mere thought of this. But the conversation flows with the wine, we get along, and he doesn't appear to be bored by stories of school. (He subsequently cancels the remaining seven dates; we are still together.)

SATURDAY 17 OCTOBER 2015

Different schools will have different structures to their leadership teams: the roles, the titles, the responsibilities. Of less importance than the number and the names is the way the team works. When we first started, we sat and agreed, as a team, how we would work together. We discussed and agreed our core beliefs and principles, the things we would hold tight to, whatever else was happening. We wrote them down. They included always holding each other to account. Not treading on each other's toes. Staying solution-focused and banning the phrase 'The problem is…' We agreed the need to model everything. We committed to collective responsibility and public backing for all final decisions, even those we hadn't agreed with. We made a list of ten things we would never be, including publicly negative about a colleague, late or cynical. We typed it up, signed it and stuck it on our office walls, and held each other to it throughout.

TUESDAY 3 NOVEMBER 2015

We have just finished our open events, a series of mornings when we show prospective pupils and their parents around the school and I do a little speech about our ethos and my vision. I pull no punches about the failings of Castlecliffe, but I am also clear on how much more we still have to do, and I talk about oil tankers. The next day, the emails begin:

> Would just like to say, I came along with a very negative view and had no intention of applying for my son to come

to you next year. However, after visiting the school I certainly changed my thoughts. The teaching staff seem to have great relationships with the pupils, and I was very pleased that the senior staff still spend lots of time with the children. Just wanted to make those points and if my son does end up with you I would be delighted.

MONDAY 16 NOVEMBER 2015

I receive a report from our Education Welfare Officer; ex-army, he works for a private firm who we employ at some considerable cost (meaning fewer textbooks can be purchased). He goes around and knocks on the doors of parents who have simply stopped sending their children to school. A mixture of threatening and cajoling, he hears some heart-breaking stories as well as many of simple abrogation of all parental duty. He gets offered lots of cups of tea.

I visited Callum O'Brien's home address this afternoon. Mum started off blaming everything on the school, saying Callum doesn't like his maths teacher or his English one or the fact he has science on a Thursday, and nobody understands him. She said he needed a fresh start in a new school. I had looked at his recent school reports and I suggested to mum that maybe Callum's attitude was the main problem and that maybe what he needed was a fresh attitude in the same school. At this point she started crying but did concede that. She told me social services are closing their case but may put in some family support, once they have all been assessed, and that dad is in hospital having a gastric band fitted. I explained the consequences of continued poor attendance to mum, including prosecution, and she said she will discuss this with Callum tonight and she was hopeful things will improve. The living accommodation is still untidy but hasn't deteriorated since my last visit. The seven-stone pit bull sat next to me in the armchair throughout, and the snake is still alive. Many thanks, Terry.

TUESDAY 24 NOVEMBER 2015

Lest I am in any danger of basking for too long in the glory of the positive feedback from our open morning earlier this month (I am not), this morning's open event gets a slightly different response. I give the same speech, make the same heartfelt pledge about raising standards, having high expectations, stretching and challenging but with care and compassion. Parents come up at the end, shake my hand, offer warm words. One lady hovers. As the room is clearing, I turn and smile. 'You bored me shitless!' she snaps and walks out. Can't please them all.

TUESDAY 1 DECEMBER 2015

Shane's mum has been called in for a meeting. Again. He has been in and out of Isolation, accumulated 198 behaviour points this year (a record, I think) and is a constant drain and a destructive pupil.

She looks at me with utter contempt. 'I bet you're one of those heads, aren't you, don't believe in ADHD.' Her arms are folded, aggressively, lips pursed.

I smile. 'You don't know what I believe about SEND diagnoses, Mrs Grayling, I just believe that all children can behave and it is our job to enforce our rules, rules that I am well aware you don't agree with but which we believe are one of the reasons the school is turning around.' I smile again. 'But you're right, I don't, in general. There were naughty kids in my class at school, quiet kids, bouncy kids, crafty ones and noisy ones. All just kids. Ones who the teacher made give out the books and the scissors so that they had an excuse to move around. And there probably are some kids who do have ADHD, but I tell you for a fact that there is nowhere near the number of kids with ADHD as people like you would have us believe, and I cannot tell you how many times I have sat in meetings with parents like you about their child's appalling behaviour when they tell me they are having them tested for ADHD, or ODD,* as if this is both an excuse and an answer, when in fact it's mostly PPP – Piss-Poor Parenting.' This is of course the retort I give in my head on the drive home. Don't want to get sacked yet, much still to do.

SATURDAY 5 DECEMBER 2015

I am sitting in (another empty) Saturday detention. I read an Ofsted report on bright but disadvantaged children. It is a fascinating if bleak read. Bright children (which I was) who come

---

* ODD – Another overused acronym which, when I first heard it, made me think someone was having a joke with me. Standing for Oppositional Defiant Disorder, characteristics displayed by children with ODD include being uncooperative, defiant and hostile towards parents and teachers and questioning rules – behaviour I imagine is quite familiar to, well, every parent in the land. When my partner found it also included deliberate attempts to annoy other people, and being touchy, he said he was going to get me diagnosed.

from a disadvantaged background (which I didn't) are statistically not doing as well as, and in some cases nowhere near as well as, bright youngsters from affluent families. If I have one thing that exercises me and keeps me awake and keeps me motivated more than any other, it is this.

The stats are shocking. Of these high-ability pupils, 62 per cent of those from more affluent backgrounds achieve the EBacc,* compared with only 44 per cent from poorer backgrounds. Yet all of them are bright. Gaining a B or higher in maths: bright well-off children, 81 per cent; bright poor children, 64 per cent. Getting an A/A* in English: bright well-off children, 39 per cent; bright poor children, 26 per cent. No less clever, just less well-off. Since getting these high GCSEs is a key predictor of success at A level, and therefore progression to the best universities, this terrible disparity risks perpetuating inequality in our society, as the elite professions continue to be disproportionately filled by graduates from the top Russell Group universities.

I frequently tell the staff, I don't want you to feel sorry for these children. They don't need our sympathy; that will serve no purpose. And, of course, I don't want you to try to be a friend to our disadvantaged pupils; they certainly don't need that. I demand of you that you do the best for these children, which is to teach them well, to deliver great lessons, to have

---

* When he was Secretary of State for Education, Michael Gove introduced a concept aimed at increasing the study of certain subjects. The 'English Baccalaureate' was a performance measure showing the proportion of children passing core academic subjects, of English, maths, a science, history or geography and a modern foreign language. As a result of introducing this, a significant number of courses in schools were cut, and it disproportionately affected courses such as art, music, drama, technology, dance, and especially so for pupils in disadvantaged areas. Nice one, Mr Gove.

higher-than-average expectations for them, to chase them up for things such as not handing in homework, to be in regular contact with home, however difficult that might, at times, be. Many of these disadvantaged children (not all) will come from homes where there is considerable poverty and hardship and where there is domestic violence (although domestic violence could hardly be described as being unique to poor backgrounds). Many will certainly come from homes where there is chaotic parenting, a lack of stability, drug or alcohol problems, low aspirations, few if any books, where reading isn't encouraged. Most of our disadvantaged children have never travelled, have never benefited from what it teaches you – about different countries, cultures, cuisines, languages, people, histories – have never had the privilege of an annual summer holiday, let alone a skiing trip and several cultural mini-breaks. Many of them have never 'travelled' to our capital, and instead spend the entire summer kicking around the local area.

I reread my favourite Sir Michael Wilshaw line: 'Poverty of expectation bears harder on educational achievement than material poverty, hard though that can be.' Poverty of expectation. A school's expectation. Our expectation. That is why we have such high expectations. We will not accept excuse or limit. We do not believe that deprivation determines destiny, and we will not allow it to.

THURSDAY 10 DECEMBER 2015

The local Family Forum was set up for schools to try to support each other in managing the most troublesome pupils and families. The two main strategies used were 'Reboot' and 'Managed Moves'. The local Pupil Referral Unit (PRU; the fabled 'centre' or 'naughty school' among the well-acquainted families) would take children on Reboot, a twelve-week programme (which we, of course, had to fund) whereby they would be educated in small groups, as well as do work on their behaviour and social skills. The other strategy, the Managed Move, would give a child a fresh start in another local school, the opportunity to build new relationships with teachers, move away from negative friendship groups and begin again. The Forum had, however, become something of a joke over the years; schools sent along support staff (who were not in a position to make decisions) and who sat round for three hours, talking about pupils who should long ago have been in alternative education, keeping their heads low when, finally, a school was forced to accept him or her (usually him) as part of a 'Managed Move', like some weird form of Russian roulette. Working with the other local heads, we successfully revamped the forum, with a commitment from the head teachers that we would all attend in person, so that decisions could be made, and that we would be brutally honest about the young people we were discussing.

The forums actually became quite interesting to attend, albeit with an undercurrent of pity at how troubled, how chaotic, how sad so many of the families in our communities are. The local PRU (where, instead of doing a Managed Move, some pupils would go on Reboot) did a good job against considerable odds. But the problem was a capacity one: the numbers didn't add up, didn't come even remotely close to having enough spaces in the alternative provision for all the troubled teenagers, whose numbers seemed on the rapid increase. There were just a handful of full-time places, where the most challenging children would be educated permanently; but for every one place there were at least twenty youngsters who could fill it. All of us were forced to contain, control and (ideally) teach large numbers of children who should not have been in the mainstream but for whom there was nowhere else to go.

The other issue was that these children would then return to families where the values and behaviours were neither modelled nor supported, so the Reboot programme was also up against the odds. All of us had wonderful staff, teaching and pastoral, whose job at times was more social worker or police officer, but who we knew were the last (often only) hope for so many of these troubled teens. Many a time when listening to LBC, hearing people phone in and say how schools should 'just kick out' the most poorly behaved youngsters, I would scream at the radio, 'But where to?!'

The final issue was that 90 per cent of the time Managed Moves didn't work – the problem being with the family and not the school. But we gave it a go, every time:

'Well, he's failed with XX, but we'll give him a go – be warned though, mum talks the talk but won't ever turn up to a meeting.'

'Yep, OK, stick him on the merry-go-round to us, but don't get your hopes up.'

'These parents are the proverbial chocolate fireguards...'

'He lasted a day with us before he told the deputy head to "go fuck yourself", but might work with a single-sex school?'

'OK, might as well, I've got all the other Shaws and Bridgintons. Be like a family reunion.'

'Parents aren't hopeful an MM will work, but we'll try her.'

'It's a shame the twelve weeks have ended. He is a classic alternative provision pupil, been good as gold with us – but we haven't got any full-time spaces left. Who wants to risk him?'

TUESDAY 15 DECEMBER 2015

Lovely email back from a teacher whom I thanked for her wonderful lesson the day before:

> Words are not enough to express how much I have valued your support both recently and generally. I know that not everyone gets to see the side of you that I have seen. You have such a soft side, both for the children in our care and for all of us who you work with. I really admire your ability to stay so focused on where you are leading us, and steer us through the choppy waters to the land ahead.

MONDAY 21 DECEMBER 2015

Letter from Georgia: 'Sorry for not coming to Saturday detention. I am not proud of my behaviour and I promise to do what I'm told from now on. Except when I'm told to do something that I really don't want to do.' But it is the accompanying Time to Think sheet that most affects me:

What do you THINK you did wrong?:

I did not attend the 3 hour detention which was set for me.

Why do you THINK that it happened?

It happened because my mum told me not to go to the 3 hour detention.

Who else do you THINK was hurt by your behaviour?

The other two people who did go to the 3 hour detention, and also you Miss, who was there.

What would your parents THINK about what you did?

They would not care.

FRIDAY 25 DECEMBER 2015

I open the last present from under my tree. Bethan gave it to me on the last day, before she caught a plane back to Australia for Christmas. It is a strange shape. Upon unwrapping, I laugh out loud: it is a bottle of vodka, a bottle of tonic and a round, shiny lime. I must have made more references to this than I realised (and probably more than I should have).

MONDAY 4 JANUARY 2016

It is the first day back. My phone rings; it's 7.47 a.m. A southern accent. 'Hello, I am calling from the Royal Elizabeth. I think you need to come and see your dad.' I am annoyed. I venture a less arrogant version of the celebrity cliché and say 'Do you know where I am?' He clearly doesn't. I explain that I am hundreds of miles away, running a school, and about to go into assembly. There is a pause for a second. 'I still think you need to come,' he repeats.

Fast-forward. Assembly taken care of, line management meeting held, taxi to the station. Virgin train to London, where I meet my brother, who has already had three beers at the station bar. At the hospital I hold my dad's hand, far more tightly than I have ever done before. In fact, as I hold it, and tears wash down my cheeks, I realise I have never really held his hand in the past fifty years. I tell him I love him. He smiles (I think – the oxygen mask is covering his face) and we grip on. Later, my brother and I drive back (in Dad's car) to the north-west. I get to my flat around 7 a.m. Sit in the bath to wake up before heading into school. The phone goes again. I know what it will say.

Afterwards, clearing out Dad's flat, I find photos from our childhood; cine films we used to watch; a letter he wrote me but never sent, when I was twenty-one and we were always fighting; a yellowing printout of the article about the school (he could so have afforded a better printer). I find out that he made several copies. Gave them to friends. One of them tells me at his funeral, 'He was so, so proud of you.' I fight back the tears. Wish he'd told me that himself. Wish I'd told him I loved him. Wish he'd had a bit longer.

TUESDAY 2 FEBRUARY 2016

Lucy comes up to me at breaktime. She is one of the most de-lightful children in the school. She loves school. She loves her teachers. She is sunny, polite, enthusiastic, pale, grubby. Very grubby. She always makes a point of asking me how my day is going. I am always polite, but I rarely ask her back; I can only imagine. She lives with mum, who is addicted to drink and drugs and has told her, in front of me, that she knows Lucy's dad 'is one of two'.

I received an email out of the blue from her gran recently:

I am so worried about my Lucy, police went round again yesterday, probably one of the neighbours called them. Lucy tells me she opened the door and said everything was fine, but I know everything is so not fine. I think she is definitely self-harming, and you lot are the only safe space for her. She loves coming to school as I know there is horrible stuff going on at home. Please, please keep an eye on her at school today.

I met with gran, a small, quiet woman barely older than me, who told me she would gladly become a guardian of Lucy ('She gets on really well with her grandad and is always asking to help him with his car') and talked to me about a 'crowbar incident' the police were investigating and about which I shudder to think. She told me how Lucy was forever saying she wanted to come and live with her, how she was scared to go home, and how self-harm was 'the one thing that blocks out all the darkness in my life'.

In the playground, I look down at her. 'Miss,' Lucy starts. 'You know for parents' evening we must have a parent come with us, to be eligible for the non-school uniform day?' I nod; she purses her lips, thoughtfully. 'My mum won't come, and I really want to come, so can I bring any adult in my family? Like my grandad?' She looks at me hopefully, eyes bright. I tell her of course.

WEDNESDAY 3 FEBRUARY 2016
I am in a meeting. My office phone rings. David, who is nearest, picks it up. He is silent, then says firmly, 'Very funny.' He

hangs up. Looks at me. I can see him trying to stifle a laugh. 'That was apparently Mr Martins, but of course it wasn't. It's Gavin. I think he must be parked in his office, no doubt been up to some mischief. Got the gumption to work out your extension though.' We head off to Mr Martins's office. As we walk in, Gavin, seated in a rotating chair, spins round dramatically and, in his best Blofeld, says, 'I've been expecting you!' He is even stroking an imaginary cat. How we manage to keep our faces straight I do not know.

THURSDAY 4 FEBRUARY 2016

I read a depressing article by a right-wing journalist on grammar schools (again), propagating the myth (again) that grammar schools are beacons of excellence, rather than just a creaming off of the most able children. I remember being once asked at a job interview, do I really believe that children who come from homes where there are few if any books, where there is no history of further education or in some cases even of employment, where the expectations and standards of conduct, and aspiration, and ambition, are far below those that we would want for our own children, do I honestly think that children from those homes can make the same progress, and achieve the same, as children from homes where reading is encouraged, where the news is discussed over dinner, where parents take a real interest in every aspect of their child's schooling? I remember leaning forward and saying, 'I don't think it, I know it. I have seen it. I believe it 100 per cent. It's harder. It's more of a challenge. It needs resilience and determination and hard work. But who wants an easy life? I am driven by my passionate belief that with a cocktail of outstanding teaching, effective management and inspirational leadership all schools can have an impact independent of neighbourhood.' I got the job.

FRIDAY 5 FEBRUARY 2016

As is the crazy nature of these things, a Managed Move is begun for Lucas, although we all know that it will make not a single bit of difference. It is the game we have to play in the system, because, quite simply, there are far too many broken children and far, far too few places in strong, well-led, therapeutic specialist school units, and certainly there is no politician on the planet brave enough to speak the truth: that these children have been parented appallingly. Three days in, I get a call from the head. Lucas has barely attended but today did show up, only to walk around the car park smashing windscreens with a tool of some sort. Staff went out to try to intervene, but he merely screamed at them ('Fuck off, you cunts' being the yet-again preferred method of communication) and brandished the tool in their direction. Police were called, who managed to handcuff and escort him away. He is twelve years old.

MONDAY 7 MARCH 2016
Email from a parent:

> I firmly believe the way you choose to run Lunsford Academy is the way forward. I know some people moan that it's too strict, the children get a detention if they forget a pen or

pencil, but my response is usually along the lines of, 'Yes, and if I turn up at the site without my hard hat, then I can't work!'

FRIDAY 11 MARCH 2016

Lesson 8: Schools should be places where children feel safe and happy. A great school is not only a place of learning but should be a place of enjoyment. I loved my own school days, and it was hugely important to us in setting up Lunsford that alongside the strict rules and the high expectations we brought fun and laughter to the school; indeed, we explained frequently to the students that it was because we cared so much for them that we had such high standards. We held numerous inter-house competitions, sporting events, an annual talent show and a Christmas concert. The end of every term saw students with no negative behaviour points being rewarded with a prize of their choice, which invariably was a non-uniform day – which we happily went along with, not least as it meant zero impact on our tight budgets. Student voices mattered to us. When I first started, every Friday I met a group of students, each week from a different year group, and asked them what was good and bad about the school; it was truly enlightening. We established the school council, so that all the concerns and complaints from the students could be heard by the school leaders. Toilets and mobile phones came up constantly, but the students could also see changes and developments in the school that had come directly from themselves. But of course, not every student's voice was always helpful.

I receive an email from a pastoral member of staff at a

neighbouring school. We have taken one of our most challenging pupils to the Family Forum, and this school has kindly (if bravely) offered Megan a Managed Move place.

Thought you might like to see this – shall I take that as a no then?! Have a good weekend! Trace.

Begin forwarded message: This is Megan, don't bother offering me a place at your school because I won't be coming. There is only one school I will go to, which is the new school in West Eastleigh, where they don't have silly uniform rools. I am not going to have a meeting with you as I am not going to waste any of my time. We all know moving to your school won't work. If you can get me into the new school at West Eastleigh fine, if not you can shove it. Megan Thompson.

FRIDAY 18 MARCH 2016
Phone Cheryl's dad. Cheryl has been a real pain all day and, as agreed, I am keeping dad in the loop. His response is factual but unhelpful: 'Thanks for calling, but I've had a shit day and I couldn't really give a fuck.'

SATURDAY 19 MARCH 2016
I go with a friend to the ballet. I love ballet. I love all dancing. I adore the arts, going to the theatre, the cinema, art galleries. I love listening to music, going to live concerts. As I watch the ballerina performing the dying swan, I think how sad and ironic it is that while the middle classes spend so much of their money on these wonderful activities which occupy so much of

their leisure time, schools are being forced to squeeze the arts out of their curriculum (and miss the talent and potential of many) by the double whammy of a narrow focus on Mr Gove's ridiculous EBacc, and a lack of funding.

In his maiden speech in the House of Lords in 1994, Lord Attenborough said, 'The arts are not a perquisite of the privileged few ... The arts are for everyone – and failure to include everyone diminishes us all.' But despite the fact that creativity is one of the most important skills for future jobs, that cultural learning has been proven to have a positive impact on all aspects of children's development, that the arts thrive everywhere in popular culture from festivals to film, TV to theatre, and that the creative industries in the UK are second only to the top earner of financial services, the number of students studying arts subjects continues to fall, and musical deprivation in particular continues to impact the poorest children the most, with very few deprived schools having an orchestra, in stark contrast to most independent schools.

FRIDAY 25 MARCH 2016
Email from a parent:

I love that you reply in person when you must be so busy. Thank you. I completely agree with you when you say get the uniform right and it's the start. We all had loads of notice and some of us even got a free uniform! I love seeing your children on the way home when they go past my door, they are noisy, yes, but they are kids after all, and the main thing is they are polite, and they often smile at me and wave. Thank you for what you are doing, from a very pleased mum.

MONDAY 28 MARCH 2016

One of the strands of our rewards policy, and one of the ways we recognise hard work and good behaviour, are our 'Opening Doors' badges: small enamel badges in the shape of a little door, with 'LA' in the middle and in a different colour dependent on how many points the pupil has achieved. I also give them out to staff, recognising when someone has done something that goes above or beyond, and I often worry quietly whether they will be seen as patronising, which is as far from my intention as it's possible to get. A teacher emails:

A million thanks for my door! I am so proud! I have wanted one for ages! (I even phoned my husband at break!) It is an honour as so many of our fantastic staff deserve one. But they are not having mine!

WEDNESDAY 30 MARCH 2016

Lucy's gran corners me at the morning gate. She looks more anxious than ever. 'I know you lot are strict about makeup, and you know I support that, but please can you ignore it today on Luce? She's put on so much foundation and eyeshadow, and I'm sure it's to cover a black eye. Please can someone talk to her at school today, try to get her to open up? She won't to the police or to the social worker.' She is close to tears. 'I am this close to just taking her back to ours, but I know that could get us in huge trouble. What do you think?' I can't think of a more difficult question.

FRIDAY 1 APRIL 2016

Ordinarily, to continue the madness of the Managed Moves system, Lucas would return automatically to the home school: us. I contact the head of the local PRU to tell him that, due to recent events, Lucas will not be returning to Lunsford but will, rather, be going directly to the PRU; he will not be passing go, he will not be collecting £200. The head is a good and sensible man, as weighed down by the insanity of the system as the rest of us. (This is in stark contrast to a PRU head I had met years before who was the epitome of a low-standards, low-expectation, excuse-ridden, call-me-Dave, youth-club culture, and who said to me once, publicly, about a student we had sent to his PRU having broken the wrist of a teacher, 'I heard it was just a slight shove, not an assault' and, 'If I excluded everyone who shoved my staff, I would have nobody left.' I told him this was a woeful implication that violence was rife in his school. We weren't destined to become friends.)

He simply says, 'Of course. We'll give him a go.'

THURSDAY 7 APRIL 2016

My English teacher Olivia beckons me into her classroom as I am on my daily walkabout. 'I think you're going to like these,' she says. The children have written their own versions of Rudyard Kipling's 'If'. They read them aloud, confidently, willingly, eloquently. They are beautiful, wise, funny, telling. Little Gavin's poem cites how one can be better behaved, kinder, listen more, to which Olivia nods gravely, says, 'Wise words indeed, Gav, and ones you should perhaps heed yourself.' Gavin beams as he nods. As I look around at all the children's faces, I find myself welling up at their eagerness, their enthusiasm, their love for their teacher. Olivia is astonishing, one of the best teachers I have ever met, one of the ones who ignite and inspire and leave their mark. I am transported back thirty years, to being in my own first year at secondary school, when I loved English, when my teachers brought out the budding writer in me, and whose words I can still remember. I have to leave. I am not sure the children want to see me crying and I am definitely sure they won't understand why. I will write Olivia a card and thank her for her genius.

MONDAY 11 APRIL 2016

I am in a meeting with Terry, the Education Welfare Officer. We talk about the ongoing but unsuccessful attempts to get some parents to send their children to school. We talk about the parenting orders that are clogging up the courts and seem to have zero impact. We discuss the pointless fines that amount to £5 a week (and are, in any case, rarely paid, and even more rarely enforced), fines that equate to barely a tap let alone a slap on the wrist. He has sixty-two open cases in our school, and he serves fifteen other such schools. 'Imagine a place', I chuckle, 'where there is no such thing as a "persistent absentee", where all parents send their children to school, where education is prized and valued.'

He looks at me sadly. 'Yes, it's called Africa,' and goes on to tell me about a friend of his who volunteered in Malawi, where they frequently had to send police into schools in order to get the children *out*.

THURSDAY 14 APRIL 2016

I am in a bit of a ping-pong with Lenny's dad. Lenny is a like-able boy, gets in a bit of trouble but not a bad kid, and dad has been generally supportive of us. I remember the first time I met him, following a brief exclusion his son had received for being in a fight. At the end of the meeting, he asked his son to go outside. Then he told me he didn't agree with the exclu-sion, and that in all honesty he thought some of 'your new rules' were a bit OTT, but that he totally supported turning the school around and would never criticise or stand against me in front of his son – 'The old school was total crap.' How-ever, at the moment he is digging his heels in over a Saturday detention.

Lenny's form teacher, Mr Simmonds, who has been trying to help, seeks me out.

'I called Mr Charles and explained that Lenny *was* in-volved in the incident, and while he understands why Lenny has been given the three-hour Saturday detention, his issue is that, as they are a split family, he doesn't want to sacrifice three hours of the time he gets with his son.' Mr Simmonds is very young, and he looks worried. I tell him that I do sympathise but remind him that at least three quarters of our students are from split families, and the rules apply regardless of the family situation.

He nods. 'I'll call him back. On the plus side, Mr Charles called you a "lovely lady" and a "wonderful head", so every cloud, eh?'

FRIDAY 15 APRIL 2016

End of the week. One of my VPs marches in, venting her frustration about the RS lesson she has just taught with Year 8. She describes the dialogue with Martina:

Martina: 'Who is that man you keep talking about?'

VP: 'Who?'

Martina: 'That man.'

VP: 'Do you mean Adam?'

Martina: 'Yeah – who is he?'

VP: 'First man on earth.' Blank face. 'As in Adam and Eve.' Blank face. 'First man God made, you might have seen a picture of them in the Garden of Eden, with a leaf over their private parts?' Blank face.

'Then I gave up. Drink?'

MONDAY 18 APRIL 2016

Email from the VP running Daily Detention:

I said I would take Shane to the toilet when we have settled detention, and that he will have to wait. He kept on being difficult, so I rang mum, but when I put her on the phone to him, hoping she'd settle him, she instead told her son that my making him wait 15 minutes was against his human rights and told him to leave. Has just walked out, as instructed by his mother.

WEDNESDAY 20 APRIL 2016

Lexie is hard work. I know her older brother has been permanently excluded from two other local schools for persistent disruption, defiance and aggression. Mum is utterly unsupportive of us. I almost think she takes some sort of perverse pleasure in taunting us through her daughter's poor behaviour. Today's episode is over Lexie refusing to remove her nose stud. As I walk past on my way to assembly, she is sitting in reception, arms folded, smirk permanent, stud glistening.

The VP calls home about the stud and then comes to my office to update me. Mum says Lexie is being difficult at home and they have Early Help and a CAMHS* referral and the doctor is also advising. She says that Lexie may have ADHD and ODD (of course she might, I think). Mum is concerned that she is so many years behind in school that she will never catch up, but says she does not read or do any maths at home. The VP suggests that mum takes her phone away for a few

---

* Standing for Child and Adolescent Mental Health Services, the term CAMHS is used for all services that work with children and young people who have difficulties with their emotional wellbeing. Although no child should have to wait longer than nine weeks to be seen, a lack of funds has resulted in a rise of more than 600 per cent being on waiting lists for such support, and in 2020 the number of youngsters waiting more than a year had trebled. In the UK it is estimated that one in eight children are affected by mental health problems, and there has been a 48 per cent increase in depression and anxiety among British children in the past fifteen years. Families (and schools) pinning hope on CAMHS for any swift support and help will always be disappointed.

hours each day and do these things with her. She says she is reluctant to confiscate her phone, she has already taken her Xbox, but yes, she is worried about how much time Lexie spends on the internet. She says that Lexie doesn't eat very much, and that she believes the school should teach her 'different to the other kids'. When questioned on how, she says Lexie needs more help to catch up as her reading is so behind, and why can't she 'get one-to-one support like my boy does at the centre'? The VP explains that, while he also thinks one-to-one support would help Lexie catch up, there simply aren't the resources available for this. (And that, in fact, one-to-one support is a good definition of parenting, he should have added.)

At this point another member of staff comes in. There is an allegation that Lexie has also brought cigarettes into school. I am confused: I thought she was out of circulation? I thought she was sitting in reception? The VP looks sheepish; he admits that at some point during the phone call to mum, Lexie had managed to 'escape' from the reception and has wandered off into the school. We go to her timetabled lesson and there she is, resplendent in the best version of non-uniform uniform that I have seen in a while. In fact, the nose stud is almost the least of our concerns. The teacher is a supply one. She does not know this child, nor does she have the confidence to challenge her, it seems. We manage to get her out of the room, but before we can start addressing the long list of sins, she storms off back to the safe haven of reception.

This time I call mum: 'You need to get up here ASAP, thank you,' and hang up before she can challenge me.

I suspect mum was close by, as by the time I get to reception she is there – sitting with arms folded in the same defiant pose as Lexie next to her. She starts to talk about the nose stud, but I cut in to explain that while uniform is important, in fact the more important issues here are the ongoing rudeness, the defiance and then today the allegation of bringing cigarettes into the school. Lexie keeps interrupting me. I ask mum if she thinks that the way she's talking to me is OK. She purses her lips. 'She never used to backchat like this before she came to your school,' she smirks. 'The kids here are a bad influence on her.'

I look her in the eye and reply very calmly, 'Lexie is routinely the most disruptive child in whichever classroom she is in, and I would lay the vast majority of the blame for that at your door, as her parent.' At this point Lexie's mum marches her out of school. To be continued, I have no doubt.

FRIDAY 22 APRIL 2016

I meet my mum for an after-work glass of wine. When I first went into teaching, my mum was so proud; when I started working in tough, 'challenging' schools, she was still proud but increasingly worried. She read the tabloid headlines of feral children roaming classrooms with crowbars while lefty teachers cowered under tables shaking in fear, having a sneaky fag. She frequently suggested I work in an 'easier' school. I would tell her often of how it was not the children's fault, how leaders create culture, how a no-nonsense approach is best, and how even the most angry and disaffected child is still a child and still deserving of love and a decent education. Finally, I think

I convinced her and now she regards me as a cross between Michelle Pfeiffer in *Dangerous Minds* and Ann Widdecombe. An interesting combination.

SATURDAY 23 APRIL 2016

Lesson 9: Great schools know the vital importance of character development, and that children learn far more than the curriculum. They learn about the things that matter way beyond school. Great schools try to build and develop children's character, instil in them values, teach them good manners, build confidence, poise, thoughtfulness. Great schools know that even if children are exposed to views and behaviours outside of school that are far from ideal, schools can and must make a difference. I would talk constantly to staff about this aspect of our mission (I preferred mission to the overused 'vision', as mission conveys, to me, so much more – a sense of a calling, a vocation, something that must be done, of the utmost importance, of duty). I would often remind them on a wet Tuesday of their vital role in helping our pupils to develop into adults we would admire and respect, of how the character of our young people will eventually shape the character of our society and make a difference to the world – and isn't that, I would ask, the reason we all came into teaching?

We agreed, as a school, on the values we felt were the most important and then we worked tirelessly to ensure they did not just remain words on a website but rather were lived, breathed, modelled, mentioned constantly, rewarded when exhibited. We sought endlessly to find opportunities to weave our values into our teaching and our conversations; our values were at the heart of every assembly message. We had a vertical tutoring system – children in mixed-age tutor groups for their structured morning tutor time, which helped to develop cross-age friendships, and where our values and beliefs were discussed through real-life examples each morning. We held themed weeks around moral issues – recycling week, kindness week, anti-racism week – but also worked tirelessly to ensure these were not one-off gimmicks but permeated every aspect of the school. Knowing that our children face many challenges in today's world, and conscious of the pernicious, poisonous influence of the internet, exposing them to dangerous views and misinformation, we developed a strong PSHE (personal, social and health education) programme, where we addressed toxic views, to try to arm them to tackle such views and prejudices head on outside of school. We had Martin Luther King's words on posters in every classroom: 'Our lives begin to end the day we become silent about things that matter.'

Email to the school:

Last Wednesday it was an awful afternoon, cold and pouring with rain, and I was returning home from the Bluedale Centre with my three-year-old grandson, waiting for a bus heading to Lunsford. There was already a crowd of students waiting so I reasoned I would need to wait for the next one. But no, not at all. One student said, 'Wait, let this lady on first,' and they all stood back, one of them even helping me with the buggy. I asked him what school he went to, but I wish I had asked him his name. We hear so much of how badly behaved kids today are, how rude, but I was so impressed by how polite and thoughtful they were. Can you maybe mention it in an assembly? Incidentally, they all looked so smart in their uniform.

FRIDAY 29 APRIL 2016

I am showing some prospective parents round. They seem impressed, the classes calm, the children engaged, the staff at their most electric. 'What is the average class size?' a parent asks.

That question again. The British are obsessed with it. I sigh inwardly and trot out my well-used lines (and heartfelt belief): 'Well, it varies, but first and foremost, the most important element in any school is not uniform, is not facilities and is certainly not class size – it is excellent teaching. Did you know', I continue, in the swing of it now, as this is a topic that exercises me so strongly, 'that being taught by a high-quality teacher over a two-year course can add at least half of a GCSE grade per subject, meaning that the same student can achieve significantly different marks across their different subjects, as a result of differing teacher quality? Which is why trying to recruit, retain and nurture the best teachers possible is my number one mission,' I beam.

They look thoughtful. 'But what is the average class size?' a voice at the back persists.

SATURDAY 30 APRIL 2016

I am in Paris for the weekend – le weekend – with New Man. It is April, warm and unseasonably sunny, and inevitably quite romantic. He is Sicilian, which is sexy, obviously, and also, having lived in Paris for five years, speaks fluent French, which is also sexy. But it's annoying, having wanted my whole life (to date) to be fluent in a language other than my own. We are walking along the Rive Gauche, I am a little relaxed through early wine, I am speaking French and then suddenly he stops me, corrects me. Corrects me! I think it is fair to say my reaction is disproportionate to the scale of the error. I shout and pout and then don't speak for the next thirty minutes, which is hard to do in Paris on a beautiful April Saturday. But as I walk along like a petulant teenager, thinking over-the-top vicious thoughts, feeling total rage, I ponder – is this what it's like, to be corrected, when you struggle to get things right? I never struggled at school, I never knew what it felt like to fail, to be corrected, to feel ridiculed. It makes me think – it's not helpful if, in your efforts to improve me, you *crush* me, you make me so fearful and angry and anxious that I give up. Maybe zero tolerance isn't the right path? Are our high expectations unrealistic for some of our disadvantaged children? But that route is too tortuous to navigate, so I push it from my mind and return to teenage stroppiness and murderous thoughts. And I am forty-nine. It is ridiculous.

SATURDAY 7 MAY 2016

I read a really interesting article on forest schools and the impact of having lessons outside. It is as riveting as it is depressing. A rural setting has been proven to reduce the symptoms of ADHD by 94 per cent. Twenty-seven per cent of children aged eight to fifteen have never played outside by themselves, beyond a garden; 37 per cent of them could not recognise a hedgehog. On average, children watch seventeen hours of television a week. Some 10 per cent of children have been diagnosed with mental health disorders, 35,000 children in the UK are on anti-depressants and 30 per cent of children are overweight or obese. What is going on and what is going wrong?

WEDNESDAY 11 MAY 2016

Jeff approaches me on his way out. His eyes are shining. 'Just had an ex-student from my last school come in to speak to me, said he wasn't sure if I would remember him. "But you taught me graphics five years ago, and I just wanted to thank you for everything you did for me during secondary school." He said how he knew that he was far from being the best-behaved student – quite an understatement actually! – but thanked me for never stopping trying to help. Said I was the only teacher in that school that thought of him as more than just a bad student or a thug, and how much he appreciated it.' Jeff walks off, chuckling.

FRIDAY 13 MAY 2016

I receive (another) depressing email advertising the services of a company whose software will (at some considerable cost) create colourful seating plans that will 'tackle pesky barriers to teaching such as low-level disruptive behaviour'. The advert begins with the statement that 'two thirds of teachers say they have left or have considered leaving the profession due to disruptive and threatening student behaviour, and for example, 39 per cent of teachers noted phone misuse in class every day, while a staggering 18 per cent have seen teachers threatened with a physical attack from a pupil within the last year'. The advert states that 'behaviour management policies alone are not enough'. I am less depressed by the statistics themselves; these are a national disgrace and should be on the front page of *The Times* rather than clogging up my inbox. What is *more* depressing to me is the clear evidence that so many schools – so many school leaders – continue to let down the staff they should support and the students they serve. Expensive software isn't the solution; clear, strong, values-led leadership is. Leaders who hold the line. Leaders who set clear rules and then enforce them. Leaders who say the adults are in charge (and by which I mean the staff and not the parents). Leaders who know that 'No' is a full sentence. How it is really very, very simple albeit very, very hard work.

SATURDAY 14 MAY 2016

A few months ago, Giles, the head of science and a passionate gardener, proposed a plan to see if we could get to use some of the local authority's treasured allotments. Many of our children live in tower blocks, and the idea of them being able to plant their own vegetables, tend them, pick, cook and eat them seemed joyous. Fast-forward to today. We have managed to find a sympathetic supporter at the council who I suspect has fast-tracked us up the list; we've been awarded four small allotments near the cemetery and have asked for parent volunteers. The children have been making some wooden planters in design technology and, despite the drizzle, we have around thirty families turn up, among them Gavin, Simon and (surprisingly) Cheryl. With a mismatched collection of spades and rakes, they enthusiastically rake and dig the small patches into what will become little gardens of delight, and which, when the first carrots are harvested a few months later, will reduce both Giles and myself to tears.

THURSDAY 19 MAY 2016

I am in Majestic (again) on the way home. The young lad behind the counter keeps looking at me suspiciously. I wonder if I am being judged for being such a frequent flyer to the store, or if I look like a shoplifter. I am not sure which is worse. I put a few bottles back on the shelf and go to the till. 'Did you used to work at Easthill?' he asks. I did, I concur. 'I knew it. I said to Billy, that bird used to teach me. Do you remember me, miss?' (I deduce that Ronnie Crowe – for it is he – must be at least twenty-nine from looking at him and doing the quick sums in my head, but old school habits die hard, and I will be for ever 'Miss'.) He carries on, enthusiastically. 'I was a total nightmare, me and my twin, Jonny, I don't know how you and the rest of 'em put up with us, but I want to thank you that you did, and I have turned out all right.' He goes on to tell me that he is very proud now that he has a job and a little girl, how he wishes he 'hadn't fucked – whoops, sorry, wish I hadn't *messed* – it all up', how he realises he could have gone on to university but that at least he managed to get a few grades. 'The important ones, in any case, and you and Mr Nolan and Mrs Davison and especially Mr Winters, well, I've never forgotten how you batted for me, helped me when the exams got nearer. It was all a bit tough at home, and I know I was a right pain but you lot all stayed with me, when it must have been easy to have booted me out. Thanks, miss!' And he beams and is immediately the stroppy fifteen-year-old I do now remember, and I am, as so often, humbled and heartened and reminded what a beautiful job teaching is, but mostly I am secretly thrilled that I am still referred to as a 'bird'.

THURSDAY 2 JUNE 2016

To encourage good attendance, we give all the students a shiny '100%' badge on their first day in September, which they have to give up if they have a day off. Children love badges. I see Gavin in the corridor between lessons. His badge is still adorning his blazer. I point at it and give him the thumbs up. He beams. 'That's not going nowhere!'

FRIDAY 10 JUNE 2016

I go to a leadership conference. I hate being out of school, but leaders need time for calm reflection, and I always come back feeling more focused and more determined than ever. I remember reading once that there's a reason why airline attendants always instruct us that in the case of an emergency we'll be most able to help others if we secure our own oxygen masks first. It's the quality of the decisions we make, not the quantity, and so often impaired decision making comes from not taking time to recharge. I know this is true. I know that when I re-charge myself, I make better decisions and am a better leader.

The speeches are inspiring, the messages clear. Open your arms to change but don't ever let go of your values. Put the health of the organisation ahead of any individual. Stand firm in the leadership space and don't keep getting dragged back into the operational side. Trust your instinct. Create a climate of opportunity and possibility. Know what you stand for and what you won't stand for. Remember that humility is a core value and that cynicism is corrosive. In the darkest days, hold on to your core purpose and values. Far better to be yourself at your worst than someone else at their best. And my favourite quotation: 'A good leader takes a little more than their share of the blame and a little less than their share of the credit.'

On the train back home, I reflect on the stories I've heard from peers in schools where leadership is woeful. A friend, one of the most amazing teachers I have ever known, who has resigned because the behaviour in the school he is at is out of control but where leaders stay in their office and blame the staff and the kids. A friend who had seen the parents of every single one of the children she taught during a parents' evening but who was still instructed by the head to stay in a chilly school hall until the end because it was 'directed time'.* A head who

---

* Directed time is the 1,265 hours that teachers are directed to be *at* work and available *for* work. You do not hear the term in schools run by good leaders, where teachers feel valued and listened to. Good teachers happily go the extra mile (or hour) because they enjoy their work, they are not asked to do meaningless things or have endless pointless meetings, and they know the enormous responsibility they have. In badly run schools, where a culture of malign militancy has developed, there is often a petty adding up of the hours and a refusal to do a minute more.

frequently tells staff, proudly, who scanned their card first and who left the building last, as if this is an indication of someone's impact and expertise when so often it is the reverse. In a climate of difficulties with teacher recruitment, these stories make me weep, but, more importantly, they make me more resolved than ever to be a great leader.

MONDAY 13 JUNE 2016

Cheryl has awful attendance: 56 per cent this year. Not through illness but because she 'can't be bothered'. When she does come in we often (secretly) wish she hadn't, as she can cause such havoc in those classes she deigns to attend, hoping that by doing so we will exclude her and she can be at home legally. Today is one such day, and she is at her worst. 'I'm only here 'cos my dad will get fined if I don't come in,' she snarls, as if expecting my gratitude. I call dad, who today tells me, 'Yeah, she's being a complete and utter little bitch at home as well.'

WEDNESDAY 13 JULY 2016

The American author Jim Rohn said: 'The major value in life is not what you get. The major value in life is what you become.' I ask in the staff survey what values we think it's vital to develop in our young people to enable them to be successful in the future. The results are not surprising: confidence, resilience and integrity. What a shame schools aren't judged by these qualities, rather than purely by exam results. I think of the wonderful events we have held this year: the spelling bee and Gavin's huge beam when he was on the winning team. The Murder Mystery Day, when through a mixture of English, science and food technology lessons the children spent the day trying to work out who had killed off Mr Jones (my suspicions would be a Local). The summer fete, a gloriously hot afternoon, when the children remembered they were children and spent hours on the school field, face painting, mask making, running a raffle and a tombola, the coconut shy, pelting teachers with wet sponges in the stocks that Jeff made for us, and a rather saggy bouncy castle which Simon spent hours on. These are the things that matter in a school, as much as the exams and, for many children, far more.

TUESDAY 19 JULY 2016

Receive a lovely handwritten letter from a teacher who is leaving us.

The school, although a building, has been on a tumultuous journey over the last two years, in which you have been in the cockpit. You have navigated our plane through stormy clouds and are helping our students, our precious passengers, to arrive at far sunnier destinations than those ones to which they were originally heading. It has been an absolute honour to be a member of your cabin crew, a team who care so passionately about the students and their academic achievements. I will always remember Lunsford as the place where I re-discovered the love of working in a school.

CHAPTER 3

2016–2017

'In the depth of winter, I found there was, within me, an invincible summer. And that makes me happy. For it says that no matter how hard the world pushes against me, within me there's something stronger – something better – pushing right back.'

ALBERT CAMUS

WEDNESDAY 17 AUGUST 2016

I am on holiday in Crete, with my mum. We have treated ourselves to a beautiful and luxurious hotel. I love coming away with my mum, which we do at least twice a year. She is great company and I know she gets lonely after her partner died two years ago. She is funny, glamorous and interested in everything, and if she would just stop telling anyone we meet about my A level results or that I was head girl, as if I had just turned eighteen, it would be perfect.

I am alone in my hotel room. My mobile is sitting in splendid isolation on a table in front of me. I stare at it. I will it to ring. David is in school, over 2,000 miles away, and it will be he who rings me as the results come in. That morning, unable to sleep, I had wandered down to the sea and stared out at the beautiful azure water. I'd thought of the wonderful team of staff I led, and of all that we have been through over the past two years. Despite the serene setting, I am a knot of nervous anxiety, knowing how much care and commitment they put into our school, our children, in trying to make their life chances better. These results have to be good; they have to be a big improvement on last year's. We are predicting 45 per cent.

The phone goes and I answer it before the second ring. David knows that I don't want pleasantries. 'Fifty-seven,' he says quietly, but I can hear his emotion, too. I start to cry.

THURSDAY 22 SEPTEMBER 2016

We came to Lunsford Academy's open evening on Wednesday, 14 September, and I just wanted to tell you how impressed we were. The teachers spoke with enthusiasm and their commitment was obvious. I also loved your presentation. Obviously the better exam results speak for themselves, but I loved the school's policy on behaviour. Please can you pass our thanks to Steven, who was our guide. I expected him to be polite and know all about his school – but he exceeded that. He was patient and tactful (when he needed to hurry us up) and could not have spoken more glowingly of his time at Lunsford. I have visited other schools since and have been a bit underwhelmed!

SUNDAY 25 SEPTEMBER 2016

Lesson 10: Finally, be relentless. School improvement might be quite straightforward, but it is hard work, and certainly not for the faint-hearted. Teaching and learning, behaviour, parents, student voice, character development, the curriculum, standards, expectations, modelling, consistency – they need relentless, constant nurturing and attention. We sweated the small stuff, always, the small stuff that mattered. We paid attention to detail and minutiae, we cared, we didn't give up when giving up sometimes appealed (though it never did for long), we knew we all needed to be 'on it', all of it, every day. It is why teachers and school leaders are often knackered (if highly rewarded) and why they need and deserve those holidays!

THURSDAY 29 SEPTEMBER 2016

There are quite a few of us in the room. Me, the Vice-Principal in charge of safeguarding, a social worker (seems a bit clueless, inevitably), the Head of Virtual Schools,* the foster parents (seem very reasonable and nice, unusually) and Tyra. She may as well be emitting steam, she is so angry. Even here, with all we are going through, it's been a long time since I saw any child look quite so furious, quite so alien, so disengaged – a word that is overused to the point that it has become meaningless generally. But it definitely describes Tyra.

---

* A virtual school teaches students entirely online and is predominantly used for those children most on the edges of society and for whom a traditional bricks-and-mortar school is not a good fit. Such schools do try to get students back into mainstream as much as possible, usually very unsuccessfully. Of course, with the pandemic that lies a few years ahead, soon every school will become a virtual one.

'Right,' says Mr Virtual Schools. 'So, Tyra, this is where you are going to come now. I know it's been a while since you were attending school, but Lunsford are really pleased that you are going to return to mainstream with them.' Tyra does what can only be described as a snort of derision, except that 'snort' implies more effort than she is currently putting into any response. Mr Virtual Schools turns towards me; he looks pretty despairing. 'Tyra has missed a lot of school, but she is very, very able, and we are very grateful to you for giving her this chance. Aren't we, Tyra?' Unsurprisingly, Tyra doesn't even acknowledge this comment, let alone respond. She just looks at her phone. I don't have any option, part of me wants to say – we are undersubscribed and this area is the latest one that has given her a foster home. But actually, what I really feel, and long to say, is – I cannot imagine how it must feel to have been moved from home to home since you were three, to know you aren't allowed to see your parents because between them they are drug users, alcohol abusers, repeat court regulars. I can't imagine what it feels like to know you are 'in care', to be so angry and empty and lonely that you really, genuinely don't give a damn about anything, that you don't care about school and you certainly don't care about my rules. But please, trust me – we are the chance you have, the only one, between a life of being taken advantage of, failure and prison, or a possible future of hope. Instead, I say, 'Tyra, we are really looking for-ward to you joining us. I know you'll be successful. I can tell you are very clever. Life has given you some challenges, that's for sure, but I know you can do well. I can feel it. And we have strict rules here because we care, and because we believe that's the best way for our young people to succeed. But it's very simple really. You will need to have the right uniform, the correct equipment, and the phone will need to stay at home.' This gets the predictable response. A sharp glance in my direction, a muttered 'No fucking way.' Eyes back down on the phone.

It actually tears into my heart, the sadness of these youngsters and their lives. I am so angry at the parents who have brought them into the world and then left them here, like this, with me and my team. But regardless: 'OK, well not to worry, I think you'll need to look at another school. That is fine. It is a shame, though. I think you would have been very happy here. We have a great maths team, and wonderful science teachers – I think these are your two favourite subjects from what I have been told? I also was looking forward to getting to know you and watching your progress. But we don't make any exceptions. I know, Tyra, [I make my voice as tender as I can] that life has dealt you some tough cards. But that's what life does.'

I stand up. Mr Virtual Schools does so too, hastily, flustered. 'We will sort this out, thank you again. Tomorrow morning?'

I look at Tyra. 'I hope so,' I say, and smile at her. She scowls.

MONDAY 3 OCTOBER 2016

I take a phone call from the leader of a school in the south-east: 'Thanks for taking the call, you come highly recommended.' He tells me he is the Senior Vice-Principal in an inner-city school and they have had issues with gangs etc. and aren't managing behaviour well. He tells me it is adversely affecting staff morale and significantly affecting results – 'To be honest, we are letting our students down. I have been told that you have done some marvellous work on the turning-around front. I would love the opportunity to visit your school and hear about how you achieved success and listen to lessons learnt.'

I am touched and flattered but yet again think, it isn't complicated. So many schools, I will later tell him, are let down by lack of consistency – in the way staff speak to students, their response to behaviour (which some tolerate while others turn a blind eye), speed of response to situations, and not dealing with issues that have arisen 'because it is not my responsibility'. One of the hallmarks of great schools is a high degree of consistency so that students do not receive mixed messages or perceive staff to have vastly different values. Such schools expect all staff to offer a consistent approach to attitudes, behaviour and discipline in the school, including matters ranging from jewellery and chewing gum to staff dress. All teachers address lateness to lessons in exactly the same way. All teachers dismiss their classes row by row at the end of every lesson. All teachers tell students to tuck their shirts in, every single time they see a shirt untucked. It is essential to remember that if one member of staff lets an incident go or has low expectations, it makes it more difficult for the rest.

Although I don't expect the Locals would ever believe it, I am also a firm believer in restorative justice. I am a strict, tough, no excuses sort of person. But when used properly, restorative justice is just a different sort of tough. I tell my visitor this. I think he had expected me to be a bit more hang 'em and flog 'em. I tell him, 'If we want our students to leave us as resilient, happy, honest and considerate, then all of our practices must be supportive of producing the sort of young people we want. Whenever we have a sanction, we need to think about what outcome we want this sanction to deliver. Is this sanction going in some way to help this child become more considerate? More thoughtful? More mature? More respectful? Restorative justice, introduced in the judicial system, was not designed to reduce offending but to repair the hurt and damage and harm done. Putting a child in detention alone is not that productive. Putting a child in detention and expecting them to write a letter of apology, and talking with them about why what they did was wrong, and asking them how they might do things differently next time, and speaking with whoever it is who looks after them at home, and building respectful relationships, and talking about future possible repercussions if they don't adhere to any agreements made – that, in my view, would be an effective sanction.'

I finish my advice. I tell him to cherish the heart, that children love praise. To only accept the best. To nourish the moral development of his students, not by bolting on a separate moral curriculum but by weaving moral fibre into the very fabric of his school. To always speak to students with respect and courtesy: don't raise your voice, avoid confrontational phrases. I know it's hard, I tell him, but we must at all times model the characteristics we want to nurture in our students. Relationships are at the heart of it all. They watch our every move, and hear our every line, and they look up to us even when it's not that obvious. I smile at him. 'Children have far more need of models than of critics.'

THURSDAY 6 OCTOBER 2016

The VP brings a fuming Cheryl to my office. The VP is also fuming. 'She's called me an idiot.'

To which Cheryl, clearly her honesty winning over her anger, says, 'I didn't call you an idiot, I called you a bitch.'

A tough one.

MONDAY 10 OCTOBER 2016

Beacon is our in-house alternative provision, one of the first things I established when I joined. It is for those children I could have permanently excluded ten times over but for the fact that there are so few places in good PRUs (and good PRUs themselves are so few and far between) that the stark (and sad) reality would be leaving them to roam the streets, or maybe end up in a dire Pupil Referral Unit, with their casual standards and teachers with their 'call me Dave' attitude, and lack of ambition. We want to keep these children in school, safe. We want to persevere in our 'not giving up' mentality, that we all have. But I will not allow their special brand of classroom terrorism to drain teachers and wreck lessons. All of them (obviously) have behaviour records as long as your arm. All of them (obviously) come from chaotic households. All of them (obviously) are angry, difficult, stroppy, poor readers. All of them (less obviously) are still just children, who need to be in a school with extremely high standards.

Melissa is one of the Beacon family. I remember the last (of many) meetings I had with her mum, following an incident that had started with a request to hand over a non-uniform jumper and spiralled into an outburst from Melissa, of angry aggression, threats and swearing, and ended with her storming out of school. Mum is pale and small and clearly poor, the inevitable initial aggression from her quickly tilting into tears and pleas for help as I hear of similarly out-of-control behaviour at home. Melissa returns and sits with her head hung low. Keeps mumbling, 'I'm so stupid, I'm so stupid.' Mum paints me a wretched picture of a home where Melissa has never known her dad and never sees him, and she tells me her own life story which has meant most of Melissa's thirteen years have been spent in a women's refuge. This is not a child I will permanently exclude. But she still needs to wear a uniform-compliant jumper.

SUNDAY 16 OCTOBER 2016

I love and loathe emails in equal measure. As someone said to me once, emails – or rather their excessive use – have enslaved the hard-working and unleashed the idiots. We have a no-email policy in the evenings and over the weekend. I read that James Dyson only ever sends six emails a day, so if he can, I figure so should we all. As I often tease my younger staff, 'Imagine, there *was* a time before email, and schools still ran!' But for all the complaining ones that catapult into my Sunday evening to ruin the end of my weekend, I receive as many that offer soothing reassurance:

I have to email you about my son's haircut! Michael's friend's sister is training to be a hairdresser, but she clearly didn't understand what he wanted and has annoyingly cut his hair really short. I was so angry when he came home. I love the school's strict rules on appearance. I showed Mike the back of his head, and to be fair he also flipped out (you know he's a good boy really), so he begged me to contact you as he's so worried! I promise you that this was a complete mistake. Next time I'm taking him to a proper barber myself.

I ping straight back:

Dear Mrs Pryor,

Thank you for your email. I also appreciate the fact that Michael wanted you to contact us; that is a good reflection on him, the fact that in Year 11 he still understands and respects the rules. As this is a genuine error, please reassure him that there'll be no action from us, and thankfully hair grows back quickly.

MONDAY 17 OCTOBER 2016

Monday morning briefing for staff. It is raining. It is cold. It is midterm. Tempers will be fraught, ours and the children's. I decide not to say a great deal but rather tell them of a parent who, years earlier, said to me about her son words that I have never forgotten: 'School is his second home.' I talk about our huge responsibility and privilege. And then I adapt the lines from Kofi Annan when he was speaking about family:

It is within the school that children learn the values that will guide them for the rest of their lives. It is within the school that they form their earliest relationships, learn to communicate with others and interact with the world around them. It is within the school that the notion of human rights becomes a reality lived on a daily basis. If tolerance, respect and equity permeate school life, they will translate into values that shape societies, nations and the world.

I look up. 'Let's go shape the world today.'

TUESDAY 29 NOVEMBER 2016

When I was at school, I used to wonder what the head did all day (and I certainly couldn't ask her, as I never saw her). Friends are always interested in what my job entails. Everyone is an expert in education – we all went to school, didn't we? We know what it's about, what works, what doesn't. We have all seen the *Educating* series. I often say, imagine the top ten things you think I deal with all day. They will undoubtedly list delivering inspiring assemblies, analysing complex data, writing reports, interviewing teachers, holding long meetings (not if I can help it). I do all of these things (not the long meetings), but in reality, it is easier to think not of *what* I do but of who I am – teacher, yes, but also parent, social worker, police officer, nurse, psychic, coach, taxi driver, therapist, actor, careers adviser, counsellor and, on one memorable but thankfully one-off occasion, clearer-upper of both ends.

TUESDAY 6 DECEMBER 2016

Email from a parent:

> My son has just come home and told me all about your assembly, and I thought I would let you know that I completely agree with the message. I have seen my boy flourish since attending Lunsford. He was very shy and anxious when he was at primary school, but now he is a different child. So happy and confident. From what I hear of the school from him, I think you are doing a brilliant job under challenging conditions with some tricky characters!! When I was thinking about where to send Terry after primary, Castlecliffe didn't even cross my mind because of its reputation, but I stand corrected. Terry started in Year 7, just before you took over. As a psychologist, I know that children need clear and firm boundaries to feel safe. But as a parent, I appreciate everything you and your teachers do for your pupils.

THURSDAY 8 DECEMBER 2016

After starting with us in October, Tyra very quickly found herself in Beacon due to her constant disruption in lessons, arguments with staff, refusal to wear correct uniform and frequent rudeness. As she is a looked-after child, we have an even stronger moral duty than ever to do everything we can to keep her in school and not exclude, leaving her to wander the streets and get even more heavily involved in drugs and crime than we know she already is. *She* would like us to exclude her; when a child seemingly doesn't care about anything, it is a challenge.

Tyra's phone has gone off. She won't hand it over, so I am called. She looks at me almost triumphantly. 'Oh, Tyra, what a shame!' I smile at her. 'You know the rules. Do we really have to isolate you until you hand it over? You are doing so well. How silly.'

'It's your rules that are fucking silly.' She glares at me.

'Please don't swear, that is not acceptable. I really thought you were brighter than this. If you don't hand the phone over, it goes on and on. You know that, Tyra.'

'I don't care.' The scowl is fixed.

'Do you know, I don't believe that. I think you really care. Really care deeply. I think you are super-bright, capable, so talented, but also so angry and bitter and very sad. And I really understand that. You have had some real knocks in life. But do you know something – we all have difficult lives. You do, I do. Most people do, to some degree. But life goes on. I really care for you, really care a lot, we all do. But you will hand over the phone.'

Later it mysteriously appears on my chair, with a crumpled note of apology, signed 'TR', making me smile and sob at the same time. We really are her only hope.

FRIDAY 16 DECEMBER 2016

I'm in a return-from-exclusion meeting. Lexie had walked out of a lesson (again), been rude to staff who were trying to contain her (again) and ended up shoving three members of staff including myself as she ran out of school (again). She is sneering, unrepentant, distracted. I start by saying how well Lexie had been doing (it is all relative, of course) and how disappointed I am in her. Lexie shows absolutely no remorse, saying the incident had been 'funny'. When I ask her about pushing me, she says with a shrug, 'You can't stand in my way.' Mum today is the least combative I have seen, says Lexie has been 'uncontrollably horrible at home', including disappearing and returning at 3 a.m. Mum cries; Lexie still shows no remorse, even scorning her for crying. Mum has called social services – Lexie apparently referring to the social worker during the meeting as a 'foreign cunt' – and the police, whom Lexie also referred to at the time as 'fucking pigs'. Mum tells me, in between sobs, that Lexie would like to live with her father, who has been back in contact in the last few months, having left when she was around two and not having been in touch since. He does not especially want her to live with him, and mum thinks this would, in any case, be a bad idea as he has no job, is drinking, and lets Lexie drink and smoke when she is with him.

SATURDAY 17 DECEMBER 2016

I meet a friend for lunch who is doing a creative writing course and is currently reading Hardy. 'Can't get into him,' she sighs. I tell her that *Far From the Madding Crowd* is one of my all-time favourite books and realise, as I do so, that it was because of Mrs Kent, who taught us O level, and whose passion and insight were infectious. I remember Mr Hopkins, who taught me that stationery (the sort you write on) has the 'e' for envelope, and that, to remember the ending of the trickiest of words, to say, 'onomatopoeia-ends-in-a', two spellings I have never forgotten. I recall Mrs Bridges, who, in our final year of school, after several weeks of coughing in lessons, stopped coming to school but insisted that our upper sixth class attend lessons in her home so she could still teach us A level Latin, something that we, of course, found exciting and funny, rather than seeing it for the astonishing act of kindness and dedication that it actually was, from a teacher who, we found out a few months later, had been in her final days. I remember Mrs Price in primary school, refusing to take my project on India when I handed it in, as she knew it had been rushed and careless and she would not accept my low standards and laziness. And the story I remember the most acutely, my primary head teacher, who I was brought to for having been unkind to another student and for getting others to do the same, who I remember not shouting at me, not lecturing, but telling me how I was a born leader and with that quality comes a great responsibility, that you can lead people in the right direction or you can take them in the wrong one. I still hear her words and reflect on that wise lesson to this day.

MONDAY 19 DECEMBER 2016

Tyra has gone missing (again). Grant, our Beacon captain, catches me: 'I'm in daily contact with Teresa [foster mum, patience of a saint], Tyra has a referral to Drink Awareness next week, something that we discussed at her recent review meeting. Teresa is really concerned about her drinking. But I thought you should know, after I asked Tyra what her plans were for the weekend last time she was in, she informed me that she is "going to get out of her face on Thunderbird".

I call Teresa to ask if there is any news. 'Sadly, no. She's still missing this morning. She's not answering her phone but was on Snapchat with her mother last night. The chat didn't end well, she told me, Tyra telling mum to fuck off. We've been to the house she's usually at, but they say she isn't there.' I ask if she's OK. 'We are as OK as we can be, with all this and Christmas.'

WEDNESDAY 21 DECEMBER 2016

Receive a wonderful Christmas card from a young teacher, who writes, simply, 'Thank you for making me feel valued here.' I am reminded, as I am so often on account of it being pinned above my computer at home, of the Maya Angelou quotation: 'People will forget what you said, people will forget what you did, but people will never forget how you made them feel.'

MONDAY 2 JANUARY 2017

I have listened to LBC since I was ten. It is my staple, my comfort, the background noise to my daily life. Iain Dale does the Drive show and I listen avidly on my own drive home. Frequently the topics include schools and education, and just as frequently I scream at the radio as someone talks nonsense about a world in which everyone is an expert. In my head I have taken him to task on many things, since he doesn't agree with school uniform and seems to support parents taking children out of school in term-time. One call prompts me to get really angry. A teacher has rung in and claims she works until two in the morning and gets up at five to carry on. I roll my eyes and imagine calling in to set the record straight: that either this is simply not true or, if it is, she must be spectacularly useless at her job. That nobody needs to work those sorts of hours. That a school must be extremely poorly run if its staff members are working every evening and weekends. That stories like this, of teachers working every evening and weekend, does such damage to the teaching profession, it puts people off joining. That there are heads out there, like me, who take the work–life balance of their staff extremely seriously! Maybe one day I should actually call in.

THURSDAY 6 APRIL 2017

My PA Claire comes in. 'There's a parent making a fuss in reception, apparently. They have asked for support.' I sigh. Another angry parent complaining that we are keeping their child in detention, I imagine, as I trot down the stairs. As I approach the ground floor, though, I can hear not just shouting, not just a raised voice, but a torrent of swearing and screaming, and then the reception area comes into view and I see its source, a young and very angry woman, and several members of senior staff trying to reason with her. It is not going to happen. Every other word starts with an 'f' or a 'c', and none of the words hang together into any meaningful sentences; rather, they are just an outpouring of abuse and insults of every staff member who goes into her view. As she sees me, I become the target. 'What's going on?' I hiss at my Vice-Principal, who is standing wearily to the side of the reception doors.

I don't know this parent. I know her children, though. A boy and a girl. Lovely. Quiet and hard-working. She is incensed that they have got a detention for a minor misdemeanour, but of course this outpouring of bile and hatred is not really about the detention; it's about herself, her anger, her own backstory, her own mental health, her drug issues, her sadness. Anger is just fear brought to the boil. It is tragic. It is also relentless. It goes on for thirty minutes. During this time we have to redirect the pupils as they finish school so that they avoid the main stairs and don't hear this abuse.

Following this episode, I really wish we could move to an appointments-only system, so we can ban parents from just turning up unannounced, and instead they will have to make appointments, like with their GP. My staff cannot be exposed to this, nor of course our children. But we are trying to facilitate more family contact, not less, and so instead I update my blog condemning the abusive behaviour and asking for appropriate conduct when in school at all times. Luckily, the negative responses are again outweighed by the many positive ones that start to pour in.

WEDNESDAY 12 APRIL 2017

The LLs are vocal (of course) but with an interesting shift in the commentary:

AD: Children have got no chance if the parents think that's ok.

CA: It says ring the school to speak to someone but u can never get through!!! Drives me bloody mad.

RP: I always email the teacher and copy in the head as well, that always works for me. Try it.

CC: I've never had an issue either with getting in touch with the school and when I have needed they have always been great!

JH: I'm banned!! I was arguing with so many staff so they banned me!!!!!!

CC: Rules are in place for good reasons!

SW: It's a shit school so glad my daughter has left!! They excluded her for two days, the smallest thing they were on her, had it in for her, even just being late to class. fucking joke!

FL: Rules were much the same when I was at school years ago. The thing that has changed is parents' attitudes – my parents supported the school. Being late to lessons is serious!

CC: Hear hear! That is exactly the attitude I was talking about. I like you was brought up to live by the rules and those are the values I try to instil in my child too, it's just sad others don't see the good in what the school is trying to achieve.

FRIDAY 14 APRIL 2017

I am reading the prefect applications. There are forty-two of them from a year group of ninety-seven.

Why do you want to be a prefect?

'I want to be a prefect more than anything as the academy has improved my chances of being a successful well-rounded adult.'

'I am proud to call myself a student of The Lunsford Academy.'

'Being a prefect for The Lunsford Academy would be a privilege. I would be delighted if you were to hand me the prefect badge to wear with pride.'

'I may not have the perfect past as a student but I want to have the perfect future as one.'

What is the best thing about the academy?

'The best thing about the academy is the fairness with which all students are treated.'

'Students like the rules, we like to feel we are going forward.'

'The best thing about the academy so far I think must be the rules, as classes have become so much calmer.'

'At first I thought the rules were a bit harsh, but now I realise why things needed to change.'

We are definitely getting something right.

THURSDAY 20 APRIL 2017

BBC Radio want me to take part in a live studio debate about grammar schools. A right-wing journalist who is also a minor celebrity will be there to argue for them and, knowing his style, it will be combative and potentially unpleasant. Local authority bigwigs will also attend, to defend robustly the nonsense that is the selective system, along with someone from the campaign for comprehensive education. It is all rather exciting and something I feel passionately about. The defenders of grammar schools trot out all the predictable arguments. The great outcomes. The high standards and ethos. The good behaviour. The journalist goes in with a particularly vicious attack on comprehensive schools where apparently children are all feral and teachers are hippies. Then it is my turn.

The trouble with this age-old debate is people confuse the

word 'grammar' with 'good'. 'Good' schools have high standards, have firm discipline, have a strong ethos, have great teaching and lots of sport and extra-curricular activities. Grammar schools don't have good exam results because of superlative teaching: they have good exam results because they cream off the brightest children! Bright kids in, good results out! *Qué sorpresa*. Although even that is a misnomer; they are not necessarily the brightest children. They are simply the children who pass the eleven-plus, the children who have had extensive additional tutoring, who on a certain day perform well in a test. I have spoken to so many ten-year-olds in primary schools who think, age ten, they are now failures just because they didn't pass and, conversely, and to my mind even more worryingly, many ten-year-olds who now have an over-inflated sense of their own intelligence and an arrogant superiority about them. Aged ten! And no, this is not the politics of envy, that most annoying and ridiculous argument of all, trotted out constantly by those trying to defend the selective system. I agree that life is not fair, and I have never believed the lefty nonsense that 'all must win prizes'. This is not even the politics of equality, or parity, or fairness; it is the politics of common sense and simplicity. Who would not want every child to be able to walk to their local school, with siblings, with friends, and to get the stretch and challenge, or the support that is required, and to get the best education possible because every school is a great school? The grammar debate is a distraction from the most important factor affecting education today – which is ensuring every school is great, every school leader is great, more great teachers are coming into – and staying in – the wonderful profession that is teaching.

I glare at the panel. And I haven't even started on private schools.

THURSDAY 11 MAY 2017

We have introduced a 'Platinum Parents' invite to parents' evening, to ensure we remember the large number of children who get it right all the time and who are at risk of being forgotten as our attention and time inevitably get drawn to those who get it wrong. 'Platinum Parents' get invited to a little reception at the end of parents' evening, with their child, to meet with me and some governors so that over a glass of sparkling wine and a cheap canapé (public money leads us to Lidl rather than Waitrose) we can acknowledge the hard work and excellent behaviour of some of our loveliest students and their supportive families. I get an email from David:

> Evening boss, just keep remembering all those lovely parents brandishing their 'Platinum Parents' invite. They didn't think that we are all 'fucking idiots'! Regards, D

MONDAY 15 MAY 2017

Tyra is clinging on to us by the skin of her teeth. Or rather, we are to her. She has been attending on and off. We have reduced her timetable. We have increased it. She continues to turn up out of uniform, other than those days when she wears it so that she can stand at the gate and smoke; she wanders the corridors; she takes her phone out. Because of this, she is currently on just two hours' tuition a day in the community cafe adjoining our building, paid for by the virtual school (or, in fact, by the taxpayer), in the hope that we can pull her back from the brink. I tell her repeatedly that she probably imagines she has more lives than the proverbial cat but that while she seems intent on giving up on herself, we are not yet going to give up on her. But the two-hour days are now pretty pointless.

She misses the security of Beacon and she writes me a letter:

Dear Miss,

I would be very grateful if you would consider allowing me back into Beacon. I know I've been a troublemaker since day one, but I hope you'll give me another chance. I know what I want to do with my life now. I want to become a beauty therapist. I know you have got no reason to trust me, but I promise I'm turning my life around and I'll be a better pupil. I want to stay at Lunsford.

Despite the bravado, the drugs, the smoking and the swearing, I still see underneath the lost, lonely, tragic youngster she is. She gets another chance.

THURSDAY 1 JUNE 2017

One of the (many) challenges when a school is not full is that children who are on the brink of being permanently excluded from other schools can apply 'casually' and a school has a duty to accept them. This usually means one of two things: either they have just moved to the area or they are trouble. It can, of course, often mean both. Occasionally such 'casual admissions' can be unproblematic, if the parents and pupils actively want to move to a school because they believe it is better than the one they are in. Far more frequently, however, they are problem families with problem children, who often have attended several schools (I met one child who had been to nine secondary schools; he was in Year 8) and with a record of poor behaviour, numerous exclusions and low attendance that they usually tend to 'forget' to write on the application form. The Trotters are two children who have casually applied to the school. Within a matter of days, it is very apparent which category they belong to. In the calm, orderly school we are building, their behaviour stands out, both of them roaming the corridor (interestingly, not together) and refusing to follow any instructions. After a few weeks, I meet with mum and read her some of the emails from my teachers explaining why Toby and Tommy are currently both in Isolation:

Today during detention, I asked Toby to stop tapping his feet. He just began doing it harder and faster. I again told him to stop, reminding him that he would need to resit the detention if he couldn't get it right. At this point, he threw a chair across the room, swept books from the desk and kicked a bin at me while swearing, then he squared up to me, leading the students to think he was going to hit me.

And:

> Tommy was kicking the doors to the English corridor, saying that he didn't give a shit, because he was trying to upset Mrs Cresswell as she had put him on a full timetable, and that he only comes into school to 'piss her off'. I tried to support Tommy and explained I would listen to him, and would he like some time to talk things over? Tommy didn't reply, and then proceeded to walk away from me, saying this school is 'fucking shit, it's shit'. He walked away out of sight.

Mrs Trotter just looks at me. 'At home they do everything I ask.' I must look sceptical, as she launches into me, telling me I 'just have it in for them'. Didn't Toby smash up Tommy's laptop, though, I enquire, politely, and didn't Tommy recently get an ASBO? She glares at me. 'They're not happy being in this school, and they need a part-time timetable, it's too much for them.'

I frown. 'Mrs Trotter, your children have been out of school for two years now. They both need an increased timetable, certainly not a reduced one, and they need to knuckle down and learn to do as they are told.' I lean in. 'I also understand, Mrs Trotter, that you have started a petition called "Get Her Out" and that you are actively trying to get signatures, but I understand that, to date, you have just seventeen, and the reason I know this is because I have been contacted by a large number of parents who are worried and angry as they love our school and see it as the hope for their children. And in addition, Mrs Trotter,' I state, firmly, 'you don't have to like me, you don't have to like our rules, but you have chosen to put your children here, in our school, where they are currently operating entirely out of our control. I have read some of the comments you have been posting on social media and I have to warn you that should you persist with this libellous nonsense, I will seek legal redress. Rather than spend hours criticising the school online, can I suggest you put a bit more time into your parenting and trying to instil some discipline into your children?'

At this point she storms out.

WEDNESDAY 21 JUNE 2017

Chris, my economics teacher, emails me:

Perhaps the loveliest thing that's ever happened to me! Have just read this on our school Facebook page. It makes it all worthwhile. C

Chris Smithson was my former economics teacher at Hope High and I just wanted to say thanks, sir, for your amazing economics lessons. You taught us about the Brexit stuff years ago and now it's actually happening!! I felt I knew a lot about the issues because of your lessons and I did vote, you'll be pleased to know (I voted 'Leave'). I remember all those sovereignty issues that you drummed into us, and how laws should be made by our democratically elected MPs. I can remember so clearly all the stuff about the economy and trade and when you were talking about foreign holidays getting more expensive you told us all about your recent holiday to Florida! Anyway, thanks again, sir, you were the best.

THURSDAY 22 JUNE 2017

I am humbled by and appreciative of the many wonderful teachers I've been able to appoint and to lead. But it's always a struggle; there simply aren't enough. I've been relatively lucky; my no-nonsense and at times maverick style has meant in general we've stayed fully staffed, but we've also had to rely on supply staff, or endure mediocrity when a poor teacher has been better than no teacher. I still get the grip of panic when one of my wonderful teachers asks 'to meet' me; my high visibility and open door mean they can get hold of me all the time, so a formal request almost always means they're applying for another job in a larger school where they can get a promotion.

When I first started at Lunsford, I wrote the standard letter that heads write to prospective teachers to go with the advert in the *Times Educational Supplement* – except it wasn't standard. I talked about how joining us was 'not for the lily-livered', how it would be challenging and demanding, but how together we would change lives. People at interview often cited the letter as the reason they had applied. But we also had to endure countless supply staff, especially in science and maths. So many of the agencies are fraudulent: they send emails proclaiming an 'outstanding science teacher available tomorrow', which of course is a nonsense. Even mediocre science teachers could (still can) lie on the sofa at home and state their starting price.

So many of the agencies are just there to make a quick buck, don't fully check out the teachers on their books, and bandy around terms like 'exceptional' and 'outstanding'. I remember one marvellously named maths teacher, Heavenly Harris, who was anything but, and could only be called 'outstanding' because she spent a lot of time standing outside a job. Equally, Ishmir Noora, who was on every supply agency's books in the entire north-west and who sent through such a variety of vague and misleading CVs that we actually arranged two interviews for one day, thinking that Ishmir and Noora were two separate teachers. We had to let her go after five days. Then we found out she had stolen two easels and had also emptied a neighbouring school of their entire paints cupboard during the two days that they employed her. We decided a more appropriate name for a supply agency would be 'Suffer the Duffer'.

WEDNESDAY 28 JUNE 2017

Cheryl is sitting in reception, seething. Her acrylic nails have been spotted by staff on the gate on her way in, not a very difficult task seeing as how they are lime green and several inches long. I phone dad. 'I can't afford £20 to have them taken off until I get my money next week.' I sigh and ask him why in that case he found £30 to have them put on.

THURSDAY 29 JUNE 2017

One of my most experienced teachers emails me:

I had a free and so was helping Liz with the Beacon pupils

in their food practical lesson. I focused on Tyra and Melissa. Melissa put bicarbonate of soda into her cake mix, resulting in the mix needing the bin and not the oven. I talked to both pupils outside about the silly behaviour. Tyra was remorseful, but Melissa just sarcastic and unrepentant. I asked them to clean a side each of the workstation; Tyra obliged, but again Melissa repeatedly refused. I warned her that refusing to follow instructions would result in her removal from the lesson, but she just threw a sieve at my head, spat and said the school was shit. After several 'you can't make me' responses, I assured Melissa that, indeed, we could but would rather she left under her own steam, at which point she did back down and went quietly if reluctantly. She was, however, muttering that the school was shit all the way.

TUESDAY 4 JULY 2017

I get an email from a parent:

My children joined you at Lunsford from Woodfield School after Christmas. I've really seen a difference in them, and I just wanted to send my heartfelt gratitude to you and all of your staff: my children love going to school; they talk to me about what they have learnt every day; they enjoy maths; I sign their homework diaries – and so do you; they want to do well. My children are learning and are very happy. Thank you.

WEDNESDAY 5 JULY 2017

I get so fed up when ineffective parents point the finger of blame at everyone else, especially since the staff they usually point it at are wholly committed to trying to support their child. I email back to one parent who is especially difficult:

Dear Ms O'Brien,

I am afraid the ridiculous story you've been given — and seemingly accepted — by Jodie is nonsense. Jodie seems frequently to be either at the heart of unkind situations or watching, eagerly, from the sidelines. Mrs Cresswell has again had to spend a long time trying to resolve the disputes between Jodie and Magda. Mrs Cresswell did not 'pick on' anyone. Mrs Cresswell did not 'poke' anyone. Mrs Cresswell did not give anyone 'a dirty look'. Your nonsensical allegations are an insult to my dedicated staff. You will not 'watch the door hit Mrs Cresswell on her way out'. She is a hard-working and devoted member of pastoral staff, highly valued by the children, and she has my full confidence. It is immensely irritating to us that she spends a disproportionate amount of her time dealing with the small number of pupils who seem unable to behave. One of your parental duties is to get your daughter to behave herself and stop causing so many dramas and incidents. I consider the matter closed.

I don't hear back.

THURSDAY 6 JULY 2017

I meet a teacher friend for dinner. We discuss whether teachers are viewed positively or not. On the one hand we think they are. People move house to get into the catchment area of a school and every Christmas and June the shops fill up with poignant thank-you-teacher cards. You tell a taxi driver what you do and the journey is then dominated by hats being taken off to us and school days memories of their own. My friend, however, says she rarely tells people she meets what she does. She used to tell people at parties that she was a marine biologist, 'except I never seemed to go to a party where there wasn't a real bloody marine biologist. Got awkward, so I changed it to backing singer.' We discuss whether, when a profession is predominantly female-dominated, as teaching is, it loses its status. We decide that overall most people like teachers – it is the number one preferred career for those people who want to change their profession – but that envy of our holidays always gets in the way.

Ah, the teachers and those blessed holidays! I don't know how many times I have defended teachers' holidays over the years. They are our perk and are much needed, and yet there seems so much hostility and resentment to us having them. There are very few jobs where work must be done then and there, no late starts after a heavy night, no three-hour boozy lunches, no leaving early. I had a banker friend who told me it was standard practice in his office to leave your jacket on the back of your chair and go off on an all-day drinking binge, the jacket the visible proof that you were somewhere around the building. Teaching is rewarding, a privilege, fun, but it is draining, and we need the breaks as much as the children do. That said, the strange distribution, and especially having six weeks in the summer, is educationally unjustifiable. More regular, shorter holidays would make more sense from a teaching and learning viewpoint and mean that disadvantaged children in particular would not slip further behind over the long summer break.

FRIDAY 7 JULY 2017

Mr Browning writes me his resignation letter. It is kind and sweet and appreciative of all we have done for him and his career. He states he leaves with a heavy heart, which I know is true, but he wants to buy a house, start a family, and these things are out of reach for most young professionals nowadays and so he is relocating to Scotland, where his parents can help with childcare, and where other children will get the benefit of his wonderful English teaching, and I am left once more with a massive staffing problem. As he hands me the letter he says, 'I wish we could just pick up Lunsford and put it in Aberdeen.'

FRIDAY 14 JULY 2017

I am showing around a friend and fellow head. Like me, he took on a school in an impoverished area where aspiration and expectation were rock bottom. Like me, he has worked tirelessly to turn it into a school where children now have boundaries, great teaching and hope. Like me, he knows what this takes in terms of time, resilience and steely resolve. It is the last lesson of the day on the last day of the week. Lesson after lesson is quiet and pupils are working hard. There is focus and engagement and enjoyment. 'You *must* be going for Outstanding for behaviour?' he asks, alluding to the now overdue first Ofsted inspection. 'Fingers crossed,' I reply (and two months later we don't, as our attendance is still too low and our exclusions are still too high).

MONDAY 17 JULY 2017

I am asked by a friend to give a talk on leadership to his middle leaders. 'You always make it sound so simple,' he laughed on the phone. In many ways, it is. Schools are complex and strong leadership is such a vital part. A hospital can be full of great doctors but if it is not run properly, people will die; in schools, it is children whose life chances will die. But it is quite simple (if not easy) and I share with the room my ten simple lessons in leadership:

1. Do sweat the small stuff, but make sure it is the stuff that matters – the devil *is* in the detail.
2. Cynicism, negativity and sarcasm are toxic and to be eliminated from your schools.
3. Never, ever, ever blame or buck-pass.
4. Less really is more: keep things simple, and remember that the smallest things can often have the biggest of impacts.
5. Never forget that the staff are any school's most important resource – appreciate them, value them, care for them, listen to them. Put children first, but your staff are the folk who enable us to do what we do. Never forget what it feels like to teach a six-period day, and never, ever care whose car is last in the car park.

6. Learn the names of the cleaners.

7. Surround yourself with different opinions and people from different backgrounds. Listen to opposing views and standpoints. Don't employ teams of talented, bright, resourceful people and then don't listen to their ideas. You don't have all the answers, but between you all, you do.

8. Most meetings are pointless and most paperwork is unnecessary.

9. Have your non-negotiables – and never negotiate on them.

'And finally...' I look at all the faces and pause.

10. When everyone is telling you what to do, and how to do it, or telling you off, or telling you otherwise – ignore the noise.

CHAPTER 4

2017–2018

'With the new day comes new strengths and new thoughts.'

– ELEANOR ROOSEVELT

THURSDAY 24 AUGUST 2017

BBC TV come into school and film the children getting their results. It makes for wonderful viewing, excited girls screaming and boys slapping each other on their backs. One child, Sheridan, autistic, chaotic home life, often tearful, often needing a lot of pastoral care and support (especially on Mondays), but hard-working, sweet, determined. Her mother was told once, 'She'll never do GCSEs.' The footage shows her with her envelope, and a knowing nod as she looks over her results; she expresses (falteringly) delight in her results, all As and an A* in maths. I am on the edge of tears all morning. I get filmed talking about what these results reflect, the hard work of students and the commitment of our wonderful teachers. I talk about how these improved results also reflect the improvement we are making to our children's life chances, and how we have accelerated the progress of so many children, including our brightest and most able.

FRIDAY 8 SEPTEMBER 2017

Leona is due to be interviewed in advance of a Managed Move. It has taken a while to get her in even though we contacted dad weeks ago. Steph, my Wellbeing Manager, looked horrified as she showed me the email dad had sent, explaining the delay:

> Being honest with you, no idea how I'm going to get there. I'm totally out of action after an accident on holiday and can't hardly move. Any way your lot could come to me? Got a dislocated knee, a colostomy bag and 500 stitches around my nethers (case you were wondering, I went down a water flume on me front, ripped me dick to shreds and the water blasted me up the bum lol).

It was the 'lol' that did for us.

Dad walks in, all tattoos and Canada Goose parka. Looks rather forlorn. Leona comes across as quite sparky but polite. I give her my usual quick questioning of when she was last in school. In one school for half of Year 6, then a move to the coast and another school. Left that school halfway through Year 7. What was wrong with it? Dad looks awkward. 'Well, I'm not being funny, but it was a feral school, don't mean to be rude, kids all off the rails, no discipline.'

'Well, we have good discipline here,' I smile.

'Good.' He nods, grimly. 'I'm not being rude, but the parents there, well, they let their kids stay out until three o'clock. I'm not really like that. Worst place I ever lived.'

'OK,' I continue. 'So she left during Year 7 and where did you go for the rest of the year? Leona?'

'Nowhere.'

'What about Year 8?'

She looks at the ground.

'You've been out of school for over a year?' I say, raising my eyebrows, although nothing really surprises me any more.

'Yeah.' She shrugs, looks embarrassed.

I turn to dad. 'What happened?'

'She slipped through the net.' He also shrugs.

'For a whole year?' I ask. I look down at the paperwork. 'So, I see that she did go to Stokefield in Year 8 but only stayed for half a day?'

Dad gets agitated and upset. 'She needs help, poor mite, she's depressed being out of school for so long, then she went there and nobody spoke to her all morning, in break she rang me up, crying hysterically, so I took her out.'

'I'm not sure half a day is enough to give any school much of a chance,' I point out, but then turn to the matter in hand. I talk a bit more about us, our expectations, about how the move will be successful if she tries hard and gives it her best. She seems to listen and nods in the right places. I think this one could work.

As they leave, dad adds, 'Thank you, she's had it tough, you know, having to spend so much time looking after people.'

'Oh, who?' I enquire, sympathetically.

'Me.'

I look surprised. Dad gets animated, now in full flow. 'Yeah, that bloody flume did for me, did the lot, rectum, sphincter, dick, everything went "splumf!" I was cut from 'ere to 'ere. Me gourmet sausage is now reduced to a chipolata. Got to have one more op on me foreskin.' He looks almost proud.

I don't really know where to go from this surprising level of detail. I ask where it happened. Greece. 'Oh, I like Greece,' I say.

'Nah, it was a bit chavvy. Full of fat, drunken cougars rubbing their bits in me face.'

All I can muster is, 'Well, you don't want that when you're eating your kebab, do you?'

These are not words I ever thought I would say to a parent.

MONDAY 11 SEPTEMBER 2017

In a meeting with Steven's mum. Steven is a delight. Bright, quiet, lovely. Mum tells me that when he joined (the year before I did) he had passed his eleven-plus but not got into a grammar school and they had both been devastated when he was given Castlecliffe. She had appealed and lost. 'Last week I got a phone call from them [the local grammar school]. A place has come up for him and they wanted to know if I wanted it.' My heart nearly misses a beat. She looks at me with shining eyes. 'I told them that no way, we love this school, he is set to get top grades in all his GCSEs and he can't wait to be the first of the sixth formers.'

TUESDAY 12 SEPTEMBER 2017

Simon looks gloomy. 'What's up?' I ask him. It seems he was

given a detention at lunchtime for poor behaviour in the canteen. 'Lunch let me down,' he says ruefully.

WEDNESDAY 13 SEPTEMBER 2017

BBC Radio call again. Will I go on the radio to talk about term-time holidays? Or rather, parents not taking them. This old one again. Surely the debate is over. If you think it's OK to take kids out of school for a cheap week in Spain, then no amount of logic and reason is going to sway you from your easyJet search. But this time there's a new appeal – they are going to put me up against the professional dad who took his right for his daughter to enjoy a two-week family holiday to Florida to the Supreme Court (and lost, thank God). 'We think it could make for an interesting debate,' they cajole. I know that my lines will drip effortlessly from my tongue, so often have I spouted them. It is not a *right* to have a holiday, and you chose to have children. Yes, it is annoying that the companies multiply the prices of every flight, hotel and package holiday by 1,000 during the school holidays, but that's a small (OK, sometimes huge) price you have to pay for having children.

'Nothing gets taught in the last week of term.'

'So complain to the governors and if nothing changes, find a school where children *are* taught, taught proper lessons, learn new stuff right up to the final bell of the final day, as they do at my school.'

'They will catch up on the missed work, and holidays are a crucial cultural experience.'

'But you are taking them to Benidorm. And in any case,

that's not the point, the point is you are saying the authority of the school isn't important, you are teaching your child a dangerous message, you are reducing the already fragile authority of the head and the school to dust, and I don't imagine you'd be very happy if your child came home from school and told you their beloved Mr Goodman was being replaced for the week by a supply teacher who won't, in reality, teach them any maths for a week, but please feel pleased for Mr Goodman, who snatched up a last-minute bargain week to Lanzarote.'

I decline, however, to go on air, but I listen in, and in the end the phone-in calls are equally weighted, for and against, which still amazes me. The debate rages on.

MONDAY 23 OCTOBER 2017

I must be the only head in the country who wants Ofsted to come knocking. They are overdue. They should come and inspect in the first three years of a new school opening. I want them to come, I'm so proud of what we have built (and are building still) and am confident of the judgement we will get. In addition, a school cannot open a sixth form until it has a 'Good' judgement, so we are scuppered until they come. I have said repeatedly to my staff that we don't do anything for Ofsted; we do everything for the children. We don't and won't do anything differently when they come to visit. You hear horror stories of teachers going home, cars stuffed with books, and marking all weekend. Every week that we don't get 'The Call' is a frustration. Today we get The Call.

Ofsted is a funny old beast. Parents will read the reports

when deciding on a school, but the reality is that there is huge inconsistency between judgements, and indeed between the quality of the Ofsted inspectors. Any good leader wants to be held to account and welcomes scrutiny and constructive criticism. Too often, however, the inspectors do not inspire confidence, often being less-than-successful school leaders themselves, and there are numerous stories of poorly led, aggressive and unfair inspections. Every school leader knows a school with a poor judgement where wonderful work is going on, and equally a coasting (or worse) school that proudly proclaims its 'Outstanding' judgement on their headed paper. (A senior HMI once told me that a local school that had recently been inspected should not have got the 'Good' judgement that it did, but that the head was friends with the lead inspector; I really wish that story was made up, but it isn't.) And how can a school, that most complex, precious and important of institutions, be reduced to a single inspection grade? However, Ofsted is how we are all judged.

After school I give a brief and (I hope) stirring speech to my staff, telling them how proud I am of them, how they must not panic, they must do what they do every day, do nothing differently. It will be quite full-on. We will have three inspectors, and one senior inspector inspecting the inspectors! We have our paperwork ready for them (minimal, like everything we do). We have polished our metaphorical shoes. Bring it on!

TUESDAY 24 OCTOBER 2017

They seem perfectly nice. Or are they smiling assassins? They

visit lessons. They speak to teachers. They have sent out ques-
tionnaires to parents, staff and pupils. They ask to see a group
of pupils; I gulp at the list of names they give. It is apparently
random, but they could not have chosen more of our most
anti-Lunsford, most difficult pupils! But it has to be the names
they ask for, and they meet with them, without a member of
staff present. I am feeling surprisingly stressed. At the end of
day one, there are some things that are not looking great. They
say there are too many persistent absentees, children who despite our considerable efforts are not sent to school regularly
by their parents (we know). They say that the progress of our
Pupil Premium* students is not as good as that of others (we
know) and, while this is a national problem, it is one we are
only slowly remedying. They say that some of our families are
very critical of us (we definitely know!). That night I barely
sleep. I lie awake thinking the worst – what if we don't get a
good judgement? What then? I have given every inch of myself
to the school, have done everything I can, have given blood,
sweat and many, many tears to the school. I would have to step
down, and hand the baton to someone else.

---

* The Pupil Premium is additional school funding for disadvantaged children, introduced
in 2011. Its aim was to help reduce the attainment gap between such children and their
better-off peers. Eligibility for the grant includes those children who are entitled to
free school meals as well as children in care and service children (in recognition of the
impact of upheaval). The exam results of 'PP students' compared to 'non-PP students'
is an important and much analysed element in accountability measures. At the time of
our inspection, 608 of our children were 'PP', 76 per cent of our student body, a stark
indicator of the level of disadvantage they had and the accompanying challenges we
faced. By comparison, a friend of mine worked in a leafy suburban school where they
had one PP student, whose father was a colonel in the army.

WEDNESDAY 25 OCTOBER 2017

The Ofsted verdict feedback session is a long and extraordinary process. Myself, David and the trust's CEO are allowed to sit in on the meeting, which goes on for three hours, but we are not allowed to speak or comment. We sit and listen as the inspectors go through each of the sections that are graded, go through everything they have found and seen over the two days, and come to a final judgement. As they speak, it is clear they have been impressed. They talk about the wonderful lessons they have seen. They describe the children as polite, friendly, impeccably dressed, and talk about warm, respectful relationships with staff. They acknowledge the incredible journey the school has been on from the rock-bottom starting point. One HMI actually wells up as she talks about the work we have done and the inroads we have made with families and the community, talks about the summer fete, the attendance at parents' evenings, the allotments we have nurtured, with parents turning out on a cold Saturday to help with our initial digging, the (predominantly) positive responses from the parent surveys. I cannot hold back the tears, and nor can David.

THURSDAY 16 NOVEMBER 2017

Email from a prospective parent:

> We were very impressed with the school when we viewed it last month and left with a good feeling. Even though the Ofsted report hadn't been released before the closing date for us to make our school choices, we decided to go with

our gut feeling and put Lunsford as our first choice. We are obviously now thrilled reading the report and your 'Good' outcome. There are some lovely comments, and you must all be very encouraged by the recognition you now have for all the hard work that is going on in the school. I just hope that we are successful in getting our son a place in your school!

FRIDAY 17 NOVEMBER 2017

11.46 a.m., to be precise. A date I will never forget. I have had hundreds of CVs pass my desk over the years; I am frequently underwhelmed. This one jumps out. With huge understatement, the HR team write in the covering email, 'Looks strong.'

I read it and get very excited. His qualifications are truly outstanding. A first-class honours degree in physics. Another degree in astrophysics. An MSc and a PhD in neuropsychology. A science teaching qualification. A huge list of published journals, articles, academic reports – *all* of them about things that I can't pronounce. He seems, quite simply, brilliant. He has worked in research, as a Samaritans volunteer, as a management consultant, in banking, and, of course, in teaching. Indeed, Pete writes in his application, 'As a "journeyman" throughout my working life, I now find myself teaching science. My previous careers have afforded me some wonderful opportunities but none more rewarding than my time in teaching.'

He goes on: 'Primarily, I am a science teacher, who is passionate about sharing its wonders with others, whatever their circumstances.' He talks about how he enjoys working with students with a range of issues such as ADHD, dyslexia, depression, low self-esteem. He writes, 'Such children could be any of us, or any of our children. Everybody is special. Everybody has educational needs. I have been very fortunate to connect with so many of my students over time, possibly as a result of having walked in their shoes earlier in my life.

'I have certainly learnt,' he goes on, 'over the years, as much from my students as they have from me.'

As well as his hugely impressive intellect and passion for teaching, he's clearly a man with many other talents. He writes in his application about the importance of his family and friends, his skills on the saxophone and his passion for music. He explains a gap in his employment as when he went on an extended fishing trip for four months. He talks about the dream of having a sustainable smallholding, and to this end, he writes, 'I started a pig-keeping course in February.' This is a man I *very* much want to meet.

FRIDAY 24 NOVEMBER 2017

When I started at secondary school, I can still remember being star-struck by the sixth formers. In assembly, they had the privilege to sit on chairs on the stage so us younger girls, cross-legged on the floor, could stare at them in awe. They seemed so worldly, so cool, so grown-up. Now of course I know they were merely older teenagers, as confused and anxious as the rest of us, just taller. But the role of older students in any school is a crucial one, representing aspiration and ambition, acting as role models and encouraging (one hopes) younger students to aim for extending their studies and going to university. Of course, in an area of social and economic deprivation, a sixth form performs a vital function, enabling young people who may not have it anywhere else to get careers advice, mentoring and an understanding of university. I remember a friend telling me that, when she was at school, she and her twin brother sent off for both the undergraduate *and* the postgraduate prospectuses (this was pre-internet) because neither of them knew what they were and what the difference was between 'under' and 'post' when it came to a degree. Opening a sixth form had long been our ambition and we now set about making it happen.

FRIDAY 1 DECEMBER 2017

Courtney is a member of our Beacon family. Courtney's mum is in prison, and her dad is off the scene. She has two brothers and it would appear that the aunt with whom they live has never given them any boundaries. Courtney can be pleasant, polite and rather sweet, and she is certainly not stupid. She can also be highly abusive, extremely rude, hugely argumentative and incredibly defiant. Yesterday she was the latter. And yet it is I who receive five abusive emails over the course of the afternoon and evening from her aunt:

I want to complain about today's events, as I am appalled at how Courtney has been treated by various teachers, including you. She was worried about her headache but was just told to stay in lesson, now whether or not she was disrupting, I don't actually care, she was scared and wanted her auntie to comfort her, instead she was refused a phone call to me. Then to top it all I've had a phone call to say she's excluded! I will be ringing your boss tomorrow to put a compliant in.

She goes on to tell me we are also picking on her nephews who are also in our school.

I ping back my reply:

Dear Ms Fielding,

Firstly, I am sorry to hear that Courtney has been suffering from headaches. I hope she is comfortable this evening. However, there are some facts you need to know. The teacher was trying to help Courtney, repeatedly asking her to sit with her so she could tend to her. She repeatedly refused. You state – 'Whether or not she was disrupting' – as if this is unimportant, but she wasted the time of a lot of staff today. We have trained First Aiders, and all the pupils know that, if they are unwell, the teacher will get them escorted to one. Courtney yet again decided to operate outside of our rules and our procedures. You are at liberty to contact my boss. You may not yet have read our recent Ofsted report, but it very specifically praised our safeguarding and the relationships between pupils and staff. It is fair to say that, as your nephews are, as you put it, 'rebelling', now might be a good time to look at yourself and the children's behaviour rather than yet again make accusations about me and my staff.

I look forward to meeting you at 8.30 on Tuesday morning when Courtney's exclusion expires.

THURSDAY 14 DECEMBER 2017

My local MP is very supportive of our school. He told me once how wonderful it was to no longer get waylaid in Waitrose by angry parents complaining about Castlecliffe, as he did for years. I enjoy chatting to him and I am definitely in love with him (which is rather pointless seeing as how he has been with David for the past thirty years). He is due a visit again, and I want him to love the school, to be impressed, to see for himself how schools can be turned around.

He is lovely, warm, interested. I tell him how I believe in the transformative power of good teaching. 'People often ask how we improved the results,' I say to him, 'and I tell them, "Well, we didn't suddenly manufacture cleverer kids. This building has always had clever, keen, curious kids; it's just they were let down, by being badly taught in the past (here and elsewhere), by poor parenting, by that most insidious danger of all – low expectation."' I tell him a story I heard once, about a child who said, 'My teacher thought I was smarter than I was – so I was.'

He later writes his blog, which only serves to further deepen my love for him:

When I was a young MP one of my favourite things to do was to go into local schools. I always gained such an insight into real education. On Wednesday I visited Lunsford for the first time since their inspection. Four years ago it was a failing school. Only parents who didn't much care about their children's education would send their kids there. Less than a quarter of the students achieved five good GCSEs – that is unacceptable. Exam success means young people are more likely to have a better quality of life than they would have done, whether we like it or not.

Leadership changes everything. Last summer more than half the students achieved five GCSEs or more. It's a remarkable transformation, so how was it done? The head is modest but, she says, it was simple. Great teaching, high standards ('We don't lower our standards just because some of our youngsters find them hard to meet'), raised expectations and strict discipline. She also tells me she sweats the small stuff and believes the devil truly is in the detail. I would add to that, inspirational leadership.

I visited lots of classrooms which were full of keen, quiet kids. A number of the teachers were recruited from the Teach First programme and were really inspirational – I didn't want to leave the lessons! The head spoke to every child we encountered as we walked around the playground at lunchtime, and she knew all their names. Ethos is the feel of the school, the invisible hand that regulates behaviour and sets the conditions under which students can flourish, and she has built a great one. She told me, 'We must ensure that we are creating the fertile conditions in which the children in our care will blossom.' She regularly tells her staff she expects them to love the children and it is clear that she does.

The school has a reputation for being strict, but I am yet to meet a parent in my constituency who wants poor discipline in the classroom. The head is clearly frustrated that this is the thing people pick up on first. 'I didn't go into teaching to talk about shoes and mobile phones,' she sighs. 'I went into teaching to improve the life chances of children.' After school, I met with the Academy Council. The children eagerly told me about how their school had changed. It was so heartwarming. Almost 80 per cent of the families qualify to be in receipt of the Pupil Premium; many of the children have very challenging lives. There is a palpable sense of aspiration and ambition. The children spoke excitedly about their dreams for when they left school – a lawyer, a pilot, a doctor, they told me. The head later told me that she asked that question to a group of girls when she first arrived at the school and they all wanted to work in tanning salons.

The school is going to start a sixth form. Lunsford now has a school we can all be proud of. Lucky Lunsford.

MONDAY 8 JANUARY 2018

It's cold. It's January. It's the first day back. We are all on the school gate. Last term we were concerned with the ever-increasing number of girls whose skirts were getting shorter and shorter. Letters were sent home, explaining how any skirt that was above the knee would need to be replaced over the Christmas holidays and that in the new term any pupil still flouting the rule and revealing thigh would be sent home to get changed. I am silently praying that all will return with newly purchased £5.99 knee-length skirts and we can get back to learning without any fuss. It is not to be.

Mid-morning. Claire comes in, face flushed. 'A national

newspaper are on the phone. They've heard that you sent home sixty kids this morning and they want to talk to you!'

I sigh. 'Well, just tell them that actually it was twelve, and that we'd explained exactly what needed to happen, and that the overwhelming majority of our girls are in lessons, learning, with appropriate-length skirts, but that yet again a tiny number of parents chose deliberately to ignore us, and there really must be more news going on today than simply "School Has High Standards".' She giggles and retreats.

For the rest of the day the world seems definitely to have gone mad. Skirtgate dominates the calls in to the school office. *The Independent* calls. *The Times*. *The Mirror*. *The Daily Mail* (obviously). I don't know why it is *The Sun* that breaks my silence, but I give a brief phone interview to a nice-seeming lady who tells me she gets it and why can't parents just comply with reasonable school rules?

TUESDAY 9 JANUARY 2018
The emails are coming in thick and fast.

> I was head teacher of a mixed comprehensive school in South Wales for seventeen years, retiring in 2001, but obviously the same problems exist today. I hope your governors are similarly strong and stand firmly behind you, as these unwanted press interruptions can be so disruptive to the smooth running of the school. It takes courage to stand firm on one's policies, but you are 100% right to do so.

I saw on today's paper you sent home students for wearing short skirts that look more like belts, so well done to you. If we had more heads like you, we might have a better society. In my time you would not get away with it, if you broke any rule straight to the office to meet the cane, and you wouldn't do it again. Well done to you. From Spain.

Bravo, Headmistress. Everyone knows the rules and if they choose to ignore them, they must face the consequences. Far too many schools are afraid to challenge students or their stroppy parents. As a mother of a 15-year-old daughter, and as a teacher, I applaud you.

And then, from the head of a school I know well and who are equally strict on rule enforcement:

We all read about you in the news. I know it is hard. But I want to tell you and your staff that there is a whole school in Birmingham rooting for you and that we greatly admire your courage. It is a disgrace that you and your staff care more about your pupils than so many of their own parents do. You are the only structure they have in their lives. And you are the only ones in their lives who are grown-up enough to do the right thing by them, however difficult it may be.

Ignore the haters and think of Roosevelt: 'It is not the critic who counts; not the man who points out how the strong man stumbles, or where the doer of deeds could have done them better. The credit belongs to the man who is actually in the arena, whose face is marred by dust and sweat and blood; who strives valiantly; who errs, who comes short again and again, because there is no effort without error and shortcoming; but who does actually strive to do the deeds; who knows great enthusiasms, the great devotions; who spends himself in a worthy cause; who at the best knows in the end the triumph of high achievement, and who at the worst, if he fails, at least fails while daring greatly, so that his place shall never be with those cold and timid souls who neither know victory nor defeat.'

Dare greatly. Onwards and Upwards! We are 100% behind you.

I will indeed continue to dare greatly with kind words such as these.

WEDNESDAY 10 JANUARY 2018
My PA emails me:

You have made the *Sun* quote of the week – 'It's a curious parent who thinks it's acceptable for teenage girls to flash large amounts of thigh.'

In true *Sun* form they continue:

Hear! Hear! We applaud the principal in Lunsford, who turned away those whose skirts were too short. Unbelievable that the parents complained about it. No wonder we are slipping down the world's education league and clearly the parents are even more stupid than their children. God help us.

Imagine if I had said that.

FRIDAY 12 JANUARY 2018

Receive an email from the US:

My accolades to the principal, for adhering to standards and standing her ground regarding skirts. Her leadership sets a standard for her contemporaries to emulate. Such academic leadership is in dire need here in the United States. My compliments.

Randy Reynolds, 6th Grade Teacher, New York City.

SATURDAY 13 JANUARY 2018

The Locals, inevitably, have a different view:

JH: That bloody school has sent over 200 girls home due to the supposedly wrong skirt. A skirt's a skirt, innit? The school needs to sort there rules out, they moan if the kids have a day off for being ill but then they send em home! Are they for real?

SW: Like I've been saying for years, that cow thinks she can do anything she likes and she thinks she can get away with it. Nobody ever stands up to her. Skirts this term, what will it be next term. She won't change. Hope they change her, and soon.

DH: Maybe we should all become Muslims and turn up in full hijab. With only the eyes showing LOL

TUESDAY 16 JANUARY 2018

Receive a lovely email from a parent after our sixth form open evening:

> Just wanted to say thank you for last night, very insightful. Obviously, we are doing the rounds of sixth form evenings and they all tend to come across as sales pitches, whereas yours was one of the best we've been to. Real passion and care from teachers. Loved our taster science lesson, we've been discussing it ever since. Fingers crossed for Colin to be able to stay for another two years at Lunsford Academy.

TUESDAY 13 FEBRUARY 2018

Tracie is in care. Not a children's home, though; this is the care of an older cousin and his wife who clearly do care for her and have rescued her from a mother and father whose drinking and drug addiction were a far higher priority to them than their daughter. I have met with the cousin on many occasions. With three children of his own, including one who is in a wheelchair, it is clear that his life is already chaotic, but he is kind, supportive and stands firmly by our rules and standards. Tracie is sweet and troubled, keen to please but constantly pulled in conflicting directions. She is regularly removed from lessons for being disruptive, and therefore often spends time with me, trying to get on with her own classwork while she cries and tells me she wants to 'be good'. On the gate last week, she told me with shining eyes that she has not had a detention in

163

two weeks, that she is going to apply to be in the volunteering group. 'I am going to turn it round, I really am!' We chat a while. I love this child a great deal.

This week, however, she has made allegations of her cousin hitting her. There is not a scrap of evidence for this and I – and more importantly the police and social services – think it highly unlikely. I think the pull of one's natural mum is overpowering and supersedes everything – including all the highly obvious evidence that one's mum is really spectacularly bad news – and, in Tracie's case, she'll do anything to get returned to her. But, thankfully, the authorities will not return her to her parents, and she is moved to a foster home.

'What's it like?' I ask hopefully.

She shrugs. 'Horrible. I just stay in my room when I get home.'

Tears prick my eyes, but I cannot show them.

FRIDAY 16 FEBRUARY 2018

Lovely email to end the week pings into my inbox:

My husband and I went to see Romeo and Juliet at The Venue yesterday afternoon. As we took our seats my heart sank, I am ashamed to say, when I saw a group of students, who I wrongly assumed would ruin the performance. However, all of the students behaved impeccably. It was a brilliant show and I think they enjoyed it as much as we did. Recognising your uniform, and knowing how much stick young people so often get, I felt I must write to you. Please pass this message on to them.

MONDAY 19 FEBRUARY 2018

I call home about a child who has been very rude to one of my teachers. Mum says sorry but asks, 'Why is she behaving like that?'

To which I reply, 'Well, you're her mum, isn't that the question *you* should be asking *her*?'

SATURDAY 24 FEBRUARY 2018

I read one of the most interesting if depressing reports to have landed in my inbox in a while, a study into educational provision across the country for the younger pupils in secondary schools, the eleven-, twelve- and thirteen-year-olds. Its findings are stark. Time and again schools, in their pursuit of great outcomes, had neglected or paid lip service to what was going on in the classrooms of the Year 7 and 8 pupils and put their budget and resources behind the other year groups preparing to take exams. These younger pupils weren't getting the best teachers. They were not making good enough progress. Their early promise was being stifled. Worst of all, they were learning things they had covered before, in primary school: they were repeating work and they were getting bored.

Boredom. Going unchallenged. Stifling early promise. These things for me should be crimes. I regularly go into primary schools and for the main part see bright, excited children who love school, who love their teachers, who *skip* to school – and then in secondary school we don't always give them the attention and the challenge they so deserve. I read on, angry and fuelled. The most worrying aspect of the report is the finding that many students became used to performing at a lower level than they were capable of. Parents or carers and teachers accepted this too readily. Students did not do the hard work and develop the resilience needed to perform at a higher level because more challenging tasks were not regularly demanded of them. The work was pitched at the middle and did not extend the most able. In the report there are quotes from Year 7s: 'The work is easy and you can just whizz through it'; 'Maths is ten times easier than it was in Year 6'; 'I don't think they know what we did in primary school – so we just do it again.' I resolve next week to spend all my time in the classrooms of our youngest learners.

MONDAY 5 MARCH 2018

Tracie is in the papers. She had been missing for over a week. When she is found, she is alive and well but with mum and dad, who are shoplifting and drunk. She is returned to new carers.

SATURDAY 10 MARCH 2018

Listening to LBC. The presenter is talking about 'the problems in teaching'. Someone phones in, they have left the profession as they spent all weekend marking and were constantly suffering abuse from pupils. I cannot bear it. Too many people will be influenced by these stories and the talented people we need will be put off working in this most wondrous profession. I gesticulate and shout at the radio. I want to say that I love going to work and know many, many people who can't say that about their jobs. I want to say that badly run schools are the fault of the leadership, just like in any badly run organisation; how more and more schools are moving to a no-marking policy so that teachers can spend time reading books, going to the gym, going out; how teachers' thirteen weeks of holiday is a well-deserved and much needed perk; how, with regard to behaviour, you get what you accept and discipline is not a dirty word; and how incredibly rewarding, fulfilling and fun being a teacher is.

WEDNESDAY 21 MARCH 2018

Multi-academy trusts can get a bad press. The badly run ones, paying their top dogs outrageous salaries and not having any real impact on outcomes, deserve all the criticism they get; good ones that want to cascade their leadership and expertise down into failing schools or start up new ones should be praised.* The trust that Lunsford is part of (five secondaries, three primaries) has submitted a bid to open and run a new school. We want to use our collective expertise and passion to build a new school, replicating our high standards and expectations. If successful, we would transfer some of our outstanding young leaders to grow the new school and attract

---

* One of the most extreme examples of high pay was when Swale Academies Trust was exposed by the *Sunday Times* in the summer of 2017. The CEO was paid £170,000 a year and four of its senior leaders had company BMWs. He was quoted as saying having his BMW made his 'frequent long journeys safe and comfortable', presumably not thinking of the thousands of teachers making their journey to work on the bus or the train, who might also wish for such luxury. The *Sunday Times* leader quite rightly pointed an accusatory finger at such self-indulgence, stating the purpose of academies must be 'the promotion of excellence, not the inflation of salaries and the granting of perks'. It went on to say, 'With many teachers earning £30,000 a year or less and some schools asking parents to help pay for essentials such as lavatory paper, there is no reason to pay administrators 10 times as much as those who stand up every day in front of a class and attempt to interest adolescents in trigonometry or Shakespeare's poetry.'

more like-minded, talented staff. It has been incredibly time-consuming and the finished bid is a 117-page document, outlining our vision, what our school will be and feel like, our curriculum, our staffing, our financing. It has been a labour of love to write, but we are so pleased with the final version. We get through to judges' houses and have to attend a gruelling grilling for two hours by a panel, most of whom look like they are on work experience. The most senior member of the panel is, however, an ex-head and tells us that it is the 'best, most compelling vision' that he has ever read. Parents have also been invited to contribute their support for us running a new school:

'As a parent, I am really pleased with my son's progress at Lunsford. I have found all of the teachers to be very approachable and helpful.'

'The school has an excellent, strict approach to discipline and has exceptionally high expectations.'

'Students are praised when they do well, and really encouraged. They are tested regularly, which in my view helps them to feel less nervous when it comes to real exams. But they also do loads of extra-curricular things too, which are just as important, and we loved the summer fete.'

'I feel that the head teacher is firm but fair and has done a brilliant job in helping to turn the school around.'

'My child feels very safe there and he knows that bullying is never tolerated.'

We leave the DfE feeling excited and positive and have celebratory drinks (out of our own purse) in the nearby pub.

Postscript: Three weeks later we hear that we have not been successful; the organisation that will be building a new academy in our community is the local grammar school.

THURSDAY 5 APRIL 2018

I receive a handwritten letter, such a joy:

I'm writing to say thank you for the certificate my daughter brought home last week. She has enjoyed school from the start, and is learning how to start each day afresh, regardless of what has gone on. Tas had a very difficult time at primary. You may not believe this but one teacher told me once, 'Teachers can't like every student they teach, and this year it's your daughter.' Can you imagine the effect that has on a child? My child lost all confidence, and she was only ten years old.

I was told by some parents not to visit your school last year, but Tas loved everything about it. She liked your speech a lot, especially when you spoke about all the fun things the school does, on top of all the great teaching. Since arriving, she has just thrived under the consistent approach of all your staff. She has made mistakes – she is a kid after all! – but she understands where she went wrong and always talks to me. I think all your teachers are great but to mention a few by name, Mrs Field has been a huge support to Tas, helping her understand her frustrations, Mrs Solomons has been very supportive about her ear condition, and Mr Simmonds is just wonderful!

I'd like to thank you and your staff for giving my Tas a great start to her secondary education. She says to me that school is her second home, and that is the best compliment I can pay you.

MONDAY 9 APRIL 2018

Steph, the Wellbeing Manager, is pale-faced as she walks into my office without knocking. 'It's Tracie.' I follow her downstairs, to where Grant is still on the phone, to the police as it turns out. He hangs up. He too looks ashen. Gives me the headlines. Tracie is in hospital. Earlier today, she ran into a local newsagent's, screaming and evidently high on drugs. It will transpire that she had been held down by two men and forced to take mind-altering substances while a teenage girl poured vodka into her on a building site thirteen miles away. She is undergoing tests to find out what else was given to her. My eyes often mist, and I sometimes have to look away, but today, I let the sad, angry, despairing tears roll, unashamed.

MONDAY 30 APRIL 2018

Pete Goddard is truly a great science teacher. He more than lives up to his CV. He also seems to have a particular knack with some of the most troubled teenagers. Two Year 11 boys in particular, Luke and Abdul, both challenging, and both with parents who exasperate me even more than they do. Both are bright but very disaffected, both rude and at times aggressive. Neither sees much point in school. But with Pete they are like two different people. Frequently they are removed from classes and Pete will have them in his lessons, where they will sit and work quietly. Today they are on the rampage; as the end of their school days near, they have even less care or concern for any rules. I know I will not have much luck rounding them up and so I seek out Pete. He grins and willingly goes to hunt them down.

Five minutes later they appear, contrite (seemingly), mumbling apologies, Pete hovering in the background. They are like putty in his hands and yet again I feel grateful and blessed by the wonderful team of staff I lead.

SATURDAY 5 MAY 2018

Despite my fierce opposition to grammar schools, I am not one who ignores the facts. I read a very depressing report on non-selective schools. The report cites studies which found that thousands of pupils who achieved well at primary school, especially those from poor backgrounds, are failing to reach their full potential after age eleven. It speaks about many gifted children 'treading water' in Years 7 and 8. It talks about a culture of low expectations and a failure to nurture 'high ambition and scholastic excellence'. It cites the most recent statistics for bright children, and in so doing paints a 'bleak picture of under-achievement and unfulfilled potential', phrases that are scandalous. Last year, in non-selective secondary schools, 68 per cent of those bright pupils who left primary school with level 5 or above in English and maths failed to get an A in these subjects at GCSE – indeed, 27 per cent of them failed even to get a B. The report cites inspectors who, when they inspect schools, time and again find a lack of ambition in secondary schools. The phrase used over and over again in inspection reports where this is the case: 'Expectations of what pupils can achieve are too low.' I remember reading the exit questionnaire of a member of staff in the first few months of the school, a teacher who had woefully low expectations and who, I had made it very clear, would be leaving us (he jumped before he was pushed). His criticism of me in the questionnaire was that I 'didn't realise that this was Lunsford, and that these children can never achieve academic success'. It is a line I really wish I had made up. And it is why sky-high expectations of our children are essential.

WEDNESDAY 9 MAY 2018

Charles, the head of history, came to see me last week, having been told the date of his grandad's funeral. It was the week he was supposed to be doing the assemblies on resilience. 'Of course,' I said, and told him we'd reschedule. He looked puzzled. 'No, I'll be in for the assemblies. It's just I'll need to leave after the Wednesday one if that's OK?' I told him not to be silly, he must take the whole day. He just looked at me.

Today, he delivers a brilliant assembly. On resilience. Bounce-back-ability. It is impactful, memorable and beautiful. The children are silent as he delivers it. They applaud at the end. I watch him bolt from the hall to sign out and drive an hour to be at his grandad's funeral. Later that evening I text him:

Thank you. I hope it went as OK as these things ever can. Grandad would be so proud.

He replies that his grandad was a teacher and would never have forgiven him if he hadn't delivered the assembly.

SATURDAY 12 MAY 2018

Apparently, 30 per cent of households have fewer than three books (and how many of those, I muse, will be the *Fifty Shades of Grey* trilogy?). I read a blog on libraries. The writer's mum was a librarian, and the love of proper books is so passionate and vivid, and the importance of reading expressed so powerfully, that it makes me emotional. 'Think before you speak and read before you think.' He is so right about reading and books and libraries. I am transported back to my mobile library as a child. As I read, I can smell the inside of the pale blue van that came to the end of our road every Tuesday afternoon, although 'van' sounds too small; it was pretty big – or maybe it's just that I was rather little. Tackling low levels of literacy has always been a huge priority for us.

Language underpins everything we do. Literacy is the responsibility of us all and is about people's ability to function in society as private individuals, as active citizens, as employees, as parents. Literacy is about people's self-esteem, their interactions with others, their health. Ultimately, literacy is about whether a society is fit for the future. We know that adults who don't have good literacy and numeracy skills by nineteen struggle to gain them subsequently. Which is why we actively, constantly, consistently ensure that the teaching of literacy and oracy permeate all lessons. We have created a library (astonishingly, there hadn't been one) using one of the nicest, most central rooms in the building, which (equally astonishingly) had previously been the staff room. We insist on a reading book being part of the compulsory equipment list. We have DEAR weekly, when for a lesson a week the whole class will 'Drop Everything And Read', including the teacher. We have agreed on a set of banned words, including 'ain't', 'basically' and, my most loathed, 'like' (with which so many people, not just children, seem to pepper their speech), and we display them on the wall of every classroom.

FRIDAY 18 MAY 2018
Email from a parent:

> A few years ago we moved into the area and were looking at all of the different schools and making the choice for our daughter, Jade, who is about to sit her GCSEs. We left your school with a good feeling but as it was your first year we were still unsure whether to opt for it when you'd not had any exam results through yet. I spoke to you and you suggested that we trust our instinct. We did that, based on what you'd said during the open evening presentation about the school improving drastically. We bought into your vision.
>
> Well, three years on and I want to thank you for everything. We wholeheartedly agree with the standards you have established. Our daughter has loved school, made good friends and is well prepared for the exams in a few weeks. I don't know why 'no-nonsense' is ever viewed as a negative, we support your strict approach to discipline as do

all good parents. I also wanted to single out Ms Jessop from geography who has been incredible these past two weeks helping Jade prepare for the exam. We want to pass on our heartfelt appreciation to your staff. We trusted our instinct and we trusted you. Thank you for not letting us down.

THURSDAY 24 MAY 2018

Tracie is, of course, still on our roll. When she turns up today she looks to have aged, even though she's only twelve. There's a new hardness to her eyes and a sneer on her face. Heavy makeup. Perhaps not surprisingly, it's not long before she's running around the building, defying everyone who's trying to help her. Between myself and Steph we pincer her into a corridor. She tells me to fuck off. 'Exclude me!' she taunts. I tell her I know she's hurt and angry and that we all want to help her but we can't if she won't even stay in one place. She screams at me, 'I really, really hate you, you're a bitch, fuck off.' She runs away and out of school. We put in yet another call to the police and social services.

MONDAY 4 JUNE 2018

Email from a visiting speaker who has come in and given a talk to the children about university:

It was a pleasure to visit Lunsford Academy and the staff looked after me very well. With such a large audience I was expecting it to be a bit of a struggle to keep their focus. The pupils were so well behaved, though, and you could hear a pin drop. I haven't seen as good behaviour as that at any of the other schools I have visited. They were a credit to the school.

MONDAY 11 JUNE 2018

Billy is the epitome of what we term 'vulnerable'. Tiny, malnourished, dirty, he lives with mum, who looks more like an older sister, and who herself is tiny, malnourished and dirty. He is barely literate, frequently absent and certainly challenging. We look after him in Beacon, our last desperate attempts to keep him in school without wrecking the lessons of other children or exhausting the patience of other staff. The VP who has been teaching in there emails me; I can sense her despair.

> Had to put 2 behaviour points on for Billy. He refused to put his tie on, refused to take his jacket off. Told me to fuck off, told me to piss off. Told me to shut up (no one likes me). Pushed open the door while I was holding it, pulling it out of my hand. Shut the classroom door and refused to let me in. Told me I was a fucking bitch. Played with and threatened to break the mouse on the computer. Threw a stapler at me. Steph removed him and I went to call mum to get him off site. I will also call mum at lunchtime and see if I can get her in tomorrow morning to discuss again. I don't really want Billy at home, as he is so vulnerable, but I can't have him throwing things at me in the room.

MONDAY 18 JUNE 2018

Week gets off to a good start with a lovely email:

Just a quick message of thanks to your academy. I am an elderly local resident, and sadly schoolchildren have, on occasion, made my experiences on public transport very unpleasant. But today when about ten pupils wearing their Lunsford Academy uniforms got on the bus I was on, there was not a single swearword, all polite and friendly, one young lad even gave his seat up for me! Never had that happen before. Congratulations to your teaching staff and pupils alike – keep up the good work!

FRIDAY 22 JUNE 2018

Sharon, my no-nonsense Attendance Manager, marches in, brandishing a piece of paper. 'Brian's dad has emailed me to say the whole family has to return to Wales for his father's funeral. Says Brian was very close to grandad and he absolutely has to go. For two weeks! Thought it was all a bit suspicious, so I looked very closely at the death certificate he had scanned across. Seems the poor old bugger died in November! My hubby always says that Wales is a bit behind but don't reckon they've been keeping him on ice for seven months!' This is an absence I sense we won't be authorising.

SATURDAY 7 JULY 2018

Geoff Barton is the new ASCL leader. I have followed and admired him for years, an ex-head who always writes with passion and common sense on all school matters. Knowing how much the lovely emails I receive buoy and support me, I decide to get in touch:

Dear Geoff,

I'm sure you're inundated with emails and tweets — especially since your arrival in the ASCL's top ranks. But I have been a fan of yours for a very long time and I have read you avidly every time you have written in TES (my paper copy, imagine!). About six years ago I went to a conference purely because you were delivering a presentation, on increasing cultural capital for disadvantaged children, and, as I'd hoped and predicted, it was fantastic and I left inspired. So, I just wanted to say how glad I am you are ASCL leader. I didn't join a union for most of my teaching career, being very scathing about unions in general, and holding the view that they seemed to get most animated when defending inadequate teachers, a curious use and waste of energy I always felt. With you at our helm I know it's going to be fantastic. Wishing you well in your role and thank you for working on behalf of us all.

And to my delight he emails me straight back, telling me how much he appreciated reading it, and that it had come at the end of a long and taxing day and how it had given him a boost. I don't think I could have been more thrilled if it had come from No. 10.

WEDNESDAY 11 JULY 2018
Email from Steph:

Tracie has again absconded from her carers. She was found on Friday and returned to them, but over the weekend she disappeared again. This time the carers are so fed up they have refused to have her back, so she is staying with a distant cousin in Lunsford. She wants to be near her friends, she told Laura (social worker). Social services have no placement available, so in the short term she will just have to stay with the cousin, but it's the same cousin that has phoned Laura many times, asking her to take Tracie away, as he cannot cope with her. I asked why she isn't being put in a secure unit far from here, away from all the negative influences surrounding her, but it seems there aren't any places.

THURSDAY 12 JULY 2018

The student survey always provides a good mixture of laughs and reflection. Last year, my favourite reply to 'What's the best thing in the academy?' was the succinct 'Lunch and geography.' We get to know who the children rate as the best teachers, what after-school activities they want more of, how the school can help them get better. 'I believe I can achieve anything if I try my hardest' gets a pleasing 89 per cent agreement rate, although the 62 per cent who disagree with the statement 'I read every night' is depressing. The best thing about the school gets a wide range of answers, from 'Getting smarter' to the frank if unhelpful 'Dunno'. Homework always causes lots of protest. 'Homework should be optional,' rants one student. 'We come to school to do work at school, and then we go home to rest for the next day. The issue is I could use the time at home that I use doing homework for other things.' 'How could we improve even more?' receives the hugely simple if optimistic 'Don't give me homework.' I sense Cheryl behind 'Stop picking on me over every little thing I do, like I'm the only person that is getting everything wrong. I have improved my attitude so stop being so fussy.'

But the general comments in the free text boxes are lovely:

'My maths teacher is amazing, he always gives me extra help after school with homework, in any subject.'

'The teachers really care, the best example is Mr Goddard. At the start of the year I was not great in science, but he will never give up on me and my grades are increasing.'

'I don't look up to my parents. I look up to my teachers and try to be like them.'

FRIDAY 13 JULY 2018

My wonderful head of languages, who is leaving on promotion, gives me a present. 'I noticed you had this on your wall, and it was getting a bit dog-eared,' she says shyly. I open it later and her thoughtfulness makes my heart swell. My poster certainly is dog-eared. It is the famous Haim Ginott quotation that I laminated some twenty years ago and have put up on multiple classroom and office walls, in various schools, over the years. It has inspired and motivated me, often reminded me on a wet Wednesday of what an important and privileged responsibility we all carry as teachers. The gift is the quotation in a lovely frame:

I've come to a frightening conclusion that I am the decisive element in the classroom. It's my personal approach that creates the climate. It's my daily mood that makes the weather. As a teacher, I possess a tremendous power to make a child's life miserable or joyous. I can be a tool of torture or an instrument of inspiration. I can humiliate or heal. In all situations, it is my response that decides whether a crisis will be escalated or de-escalated and a child humanized or dehumanized.

SUNDAY 15 JULY 2018

The end of a term can see an increase in challenging behaviour in schools like ours that serve the disadvantaged. For those children where home is not their haven, for whom indeed school is the safe harbour, the oasis of calm in their troubled lives, the prospect of it not being there can increase their anxiety and this plays out in poor behaviour, which at least gets them some attention. I have seen it happen every term, for ever. For so many children – so many of our children – there won't be a trip to Disneyland, two weeks in the sun, trips to London. There will be domestic violence they can't escape from, parents involving them in criminal activities, drugs, alcohol, poverty, boredom, temptation. I have never – will never – excuse poor kids for getting into crime, never regard boredom as a justification for vandalism or a chaotic home life as a reason to misbehave. But it adds a certain context; and tonight, while I'm being wined and dined by the Sicilian man, I overhear a child in a swanky restaurant say, 'Does the lobster bisque have paprika in it?' and it reminds me that I would never want to work in any other type of school.

THURSDAY 26 JULY 2018

I receive my favourite ever leaving card:

> When I started here at Lunsford, I was in danger of becoming one of that sad statistic: a teacher leaving the profession within five years. Your inspirational leadership, your exemplary standards and your passionate love and determined care have allowed me to flourish. You have shown me what it means to cherish this profession, how important it is to be principled and unfaltering, and why 'no excuses' is the best attitude we can afford our students. You have inspired me to believe, to focus on the detail, to hold the line, to question the bullshit, to know when to be firm, when to be compassionate and when to speak the truth. Thank you for showing that a good teacher is more than a lesson plan and a great leader is more than a boss.

CHAPTER 5

2018–2019

> *'You never know how strong you are until*
> *being strong is your only choice.'*
> BOB MARLEY

THURSDAY 23 AUGUST 2018

I am on holiday (obviously) and receive an email from a lovely parent with whom I have had several meetings. Her son is bright and well brought up but has at times got in with the wrong crowd, and between us we have worked hard to keep him focused. He has today picked up his GCSE results:

We wanted to share our pride and happiness, since you have played such a part in it. We can't thank you enough for the guidance and encouragement you have shown to Trevor, not just this year but throughout his time at Lunsford. He is pleased with his results and especially the 9 in English, especially after all we went through! I hope you are having a relaxing holiday, teachers so deserve to. I thank all your staff from the bottom of my heart, we have been so grateful for all the kindness and care. Trevor also sends his special thanks, he owes you so much, as do we all. Sheila.

MONDAY 3 SEPTEMBER 2018

Watching the proud pioneers of our brand-new sixth form arrive is humbling. I can sense their excitement, their nervousness. They are so smart, the boys in brand-new suits and the girls resplendent in smart business attire. Steven is the proudest of them all. They are such a visible manifestation of our ambition and aspiration; it will be several weeks before I can look at them and not get a lump in my throat.

MONDAY 10 SEPTEMBER 2018

Pete pops by to see me.

'How was the summer?' I ask.

'Not great,' he smiles with massive understatement. The deep depression he got through two years ago has come back with a vengeance. The counselling is good, though. I tell him that of course he must take whatever time off he needs; he grins at me. 'No way! I'm getting those attendance chocolates again.'

MONDAY 17 SEPTEMBER 2018

Charlene is an extreme child. Extreme in size. Extreme in behaviour. Extreme in sadness. She has come to us having been booted out of three primary schools. Despite all the nonsense spoken by the media experts, it is not (nor should it be) easy to permanently exclude any child, let alone from primary school. For this to have happened means two things; the school has exhausted all its support and patience of its staff, and the child's behaviour must have been appalling, and repeatedly so. Three permanent exclusions are astonishing and rare. But I can anticipate what we will encounter.

We start her off slowly, working one-to-one with my marvellous SENCO* – this is not a human grenade I am going to throw into a mainstream classroom yet.

Today, however, things have already gone spectacularly badly. Email from SENCO:

At the beginning of lesson two, Steph escorted Charlene to my office. We discussed the literacy she had been working on. I told her we would do some maths. She was upset as it's getting harder and she does not want to do it any more. I spoke about not giving up. If she did Times Table Rock Stars for ten minutes it would be almost time for her to play table tennis. She still refused, saying, 'No, No,' in a baby voice, then, 'Fuck off, this is shit,' loudly. I suggested more reading, working on a project of her choice, another maths topic. She just swore each time I spoke. I told her she needed to calm down. She said she did not agree to anything in the meeting with all the 'fat cunts' and that 'this school is fucking shit', then started throwing chairs around. Steph came in and tried to calm her, but she then directed her anger at Steph. She was

---

* SENCO stands for a school's special educational needs co-ordinator.

punching walls and lockers. Hitting her head on the wall. She also twice threatened to 'burn this fucking school down and everyone in it'.

Mum arrives for our meeting. Charlene sits in too. She sucks her thumb. She currently looks sweet and innocent, childlike (which she is, of course). 'Mrs Irons,' I begin, 'I am afraid it has not been a good morning.' I glance at the clock; it is only 9.35. I resume: 'She has been swearing a lot, F and C, throwing things around, being very violent, and of course a risk to herself and others.' I wait; I rather feel she needs to explain rather than me just describe. She shrugs; tells me Charlene says 'fucking cunt' to everyone. She is calm. I tell her I applaud her, that I would find that very hard and certainly hard to stay calm. I venture, 'Why is she like that, do you think?'

At this point she explodes. 'I am not going to be spoken to like that. I have had this since she was two! Are you saying it's my fault? She is Jekyll and Hyde: she'll be swearing at me one minute, hitting the walls, and the next she'll be sitting on the bed with me and kissing me.' She breaks into sobs, her anger at me dissipated. It is a very sad scene; I don't feel sorry for her, I just feel very sad for them both.

TUESDAY 18 SEPTEMBER 2018

'A new day, a fresh start,' I tell Charlene, smiling. She trots off happily with Steph, my wonderfully patient Wellbeing Manager. I cross my fingers.

9.59 a.m., email from Steph to the senior team:

I had given her a workbook to work through but ten minutes later she was calling me a 'fucking cunt'. I stayed completely calm and didn't raise my voice or tell her off for swearing, simply asked her to sit up and do a bit of work. I offered table tennis again as a carrot, to help calm her down, to no avail. She was in and out of the Isolation area, repeatedly swearing etc. Apologies to those who have taken the brunt of her abuse.

Email from VP:

I collected Charlene from Isolation. She ripped up her work and threw it at me, saying, 'I'm not doing your fucking work.' She did not follow me but instead ran to reception to walk out, but we still had her bag. She kept shouting, 'Give me my fucking stuff, I want my stuff.' She continued to scream and kicked over a chair in reception. I called mum, who said she would come in thirty mins to assist. Charlene is now cooling down outside my office. By which I mean, every now and then she's shouting things like 'fuck this school' and 'no! I want to go home!' and generally having a bit of a hissy fit. Steph, please add anything I've missed.

FRIDAY 21 SEPTEMBER 2018

'Things going OK with Charlene?' I ask Steph. 'I haven't heard of any more incidents this week?'

'No, she's not been in since Tuesday.'

My heart sinks.

SATURDAY 22 SEPTEMBER 2018

I watch a programme on truancy and the rise in the number of parents opting for elective home education. In 99 per cent of the cases this is parents removing pupils before they are pushed – children whose behaviour has been so poor, for so long, and where the school has exhausted all its strategies (and certainly exhausted all of its staff), where several Managed Moves have been tried, and there are no further options if a school wishes to maintain order. I wonder when the term 'school refuser' became acceptable parlance. I wonder if I can become a 'tax payment refuser' or a 'putting the bins out refuser'? More questions: Why did *social* media herald the start of so much *anti-social* behaviour? When did 'essential social services' become so essential, and family responsibility so sidelined? When did saying things like this make you extreme, rather than decent, caring, serious and dutiful?

MONDAY 24 SEPTEMBER 2018

Charlene finally makes an appearance; it is not a good one. This time I ring Charlene's dad. 'Mr Irons, I am afraid it is yet another bad morning, we need you to come up – again.' He is not supportive today, tells me he doesn't know why 'youse lot' can't control her. 'She's only eleven.'

'Yes,' I say. 'It is true, sir, we *can't* control her. We would need a lasso to do so as currently she is rampaging around the building. Swearing. Calling us all fucking cunts.'

Pause. 'That's not good. She's kicking off then?'

This is, I suggest, fair to say, although to say she *has* kicked off would be more accurate. Dad says he can't get there yet and I tell him that in that case we will have to call the police, as she is a serious danger to herself and others. He tells me he's on his way.

In fact, it is again mum who arrives ten minutes later – I think dad has abrogated that responsibility to her rather swiftly. Mum asks Charlene to come with her, but she refuses. Mum tells her she is fed up with her too and is going to call the police herself, she is bored with having to come up to the school all the time. Mum is crying. I ask her if she's OK, rather pointlessly. She shouts at me, through her sobs. She doesn't want our pity or for us to feel sorry for her. She thanks us for what we have been trying to do but says she won't be returning. Charlene eventually leaves with mum, quietly.

We never see her again. Mum removes her from our roll. I often wonder where she is and what she is doing now.

TUESDAY 25 SEPTEMBER 2018

An announcement of another addition to the curriculum: we are now expected to teach First Aid. So, on top of English, maths, biology, physics, chemistry, geography, history, RS, citizenship, product design, cookery, sport, art, dance, drama, music, textiles, graphics, economics, and having already had to include sex education, internet safety, politics, healthy living, relationships, money management – we now have to teach them to use the recovery position and treat a burn. I think, when does the curriculum stop and when does parenting start?

TUESDAY 2 OCTOBER 2018

Today, the Locals are upset about coats:

SW: What next, can you believe – that bloody school has only got teachers standing at the gate of Lunsford with arms full of coats their taking off the kids if not the right colour!!! It's 1 degrees! Who gives a fuck what colour coat they are wearing!

OY: Wtf they have a rool about the coat colour? If there asking for coats and taking them its theft.

DH: They can only wear black coats I think. Racism towards coats!! Why can't they all be treated equal.

JJ: Look you lot, it clearly says on the school website and us parents are always told what is allowed and what isn't. My child wouldn't of had his coat taken away because I listen to the rules, maybe this is what other parents should be doing! (Helpfully, TC then posts the picture of acceptable coats!)

CC: Yeah, I agree, what a surprise, buy your child something that breaks school rules and then say it's unfair when something is enforced. Rules is rules.

OY: But isn't it part of a childs human rights to be warm?

JJ: It's a life's lesson, if I turn up at work not dressed right I get sent home with no pay, and guess what, I wouldn't do it again, lesson learnt!!

THURSDAY 4 OCTOBER 2018

Pete and our young trainee teacher Sean have formed a touchingly unusual friendship. Sean has a natural flair for teaching, a wonderful way with the children and a total lack of interest in the paperwork he has to do to get qualified. There is an almost twenty-year age gap between them, but their shared passion for science has developed into a strong and trusting bond. Pete supports Sean with doing the endless bureaucracy associated with his training provider, and Sean in turn gives support and strength to Pete as he battles his illness. I suspect they share one or two glasses of an evening too, but who can blame either of them?

FRIDAY 9 NOVEMBER 2018

Receive a letter from the Understanding Gender Development Group about Andrew, who is in Year 8. I am informed that 'Andrew does not currently identify as transgender' but that he 'prefers to express in a more neutral way' and that 'the reinforcement of stereotypes through your school having such a firm uniform policy is causing significant distress'. I am advised that if the situation is 'left unaddressed', over time he will 'internalise a negative sense of his difference, leading to feelings of increased shame, which may then be internalised concretely in his body, and the normal adolescent process of exploration may be prematurely curtailed, forcing Andrew to "choose" a narrowly defined binary gender'. On the other hand, if I will allow him 'greater freedom by making adjustments to the existing uniform policy, he will feel much safer to explore his sense of self' and apparently this would mean that a 'whole new world of possibilities of how to be a young man would appear'.

I wonder what the Locals – not known for their tolerance – would make of this, although it also occurs to me that, somewhat ironically, Andrew's counsellor and the Locals both, in fact, want the same thing: to ignore our rules, albeit for different reasons.

MONDAY 12 NOVEMBER 2018

'Lisa's mum is in reception and is on her way up.' Words from my receptionist that always send a slight shiver of 'here-we-go-again-itis' down my spine. Lisa has two very different sides to her (like so many children), at times polite and bubbly and then becoming angry and uncontrollable in a second, usually over a very slight misdemeanour which always ends with her flouncing off home. I rather suspect that at home our rules don't quite get the support from her mum that we might hope for. 'Your fucking stupid rules in your fucking stupid school' being something of a clue as mum bursts angrily into my office. Today it is over earrings.

'Who do you think you are?' mum spits at me, a rhetorical if rather surprising question. 'You think you're so important, you and your...' – at this point her voices changes to a cross between Hyacinth Bucket and the Queen, which I can only imagine is intended to be an insulting imitation of my voice – '...stupid rules. I've told my daughter to ignore you and your staff, and not to obey your petty rules.'

'That is quite unhelpful, Ms Evans,' I attempt, but it's too late, as, with one last jeering snort at me, accompanied by a look of unadulterated contempt, she grabs her daughter's hand and pulls her out of the office.

I've had many such confrontations, usually far worse. I know what we are doing is the right thing, I know she is not representative of the overwhelming majority of our parents, but for some reason, whether through lack of sleep or the particularly nasty look she gave me on departure, tears well up in my eyes. Not for the first time, I ask myself if it's worth it, if I shouldn't actually look for an easier, safer job in an easier, safer area. Maybe my mum is right. There's a knock on the door and I barely have time to wipe the tears away and mumble, 'Come in' before Steven walks in.

'How's your day, miss?' he cheerily enquires.

'Fine, Steven. Yours?' I reply.

'Great thanks, miss. I've decided – I'm definitely going to apply for uni. Been thinking about what you said. I know it's a long shot, getting into Oxbridge, but I'm going to give it a try.' He is beaming. So am I. My mum is, in fact, wrong.

THURSDAY 13 DECEMBER 2018

Jeff calls me in the car on my way to work. Unusual. I answer. He tells me he is concerned about Pete: they've just shared a morning coffee and he seemed a bit odd. Odd how, I ask? 'Well, a bit out of it, a bit fragile, he did say that his friend thinks he may have had a mini stroke last night,' I slowly, firmly tell Jeff to get off the phone to me, to call an ambulance, that the one thing I do know about strokes (my aunt having had one earlier this year) is that time is everything. I hang up.

When I get to school, things have progressed. Pete was unwilling to 'cause a fuss' but did concede to Jeff driving him back home, and an ambulance is on its way to his home address. He is subsequently taken to hospital, where it is confirmed he has in fact got a stage 4 brain tumour. I speak to him that afternoon. His first words are to apologise. Biting back tears, I tell him to be quiet, but if he thinks he is going to get the end-of-term attendance chocolates now, he can forget it. We both laugh. Later I text Sean, who's visiting him in hospital. He replies, 'He's in good spirits and in thirty minutes he's going home with a new walking stick!' Later still he sends me a lovely picture of Pete by his fish tank, looking relaxed in his slippers.

SUNDAY 16 DECEMBER 2018

Voice message from Sean, 8.59 p.m.: 'Pete's had another massive seizure. I'm on the way to hospital, but it doesn't look good. He's unconscious.'

I text simply: 'I'm praying for you both.'

MONDAY 17 DECEMBER 2018

Voicemail from Sean in the middle of the night telling me he's still at the hospital, by his bedside, and that Pete has swelling around the tumour. He ends the message, 'I'll be in tomorrow.'

Life – and school, it seems – must go on.

TUESDAY 18 DECEMBER 2018

Courtney and Dawn are both now Beacon ladies. I like them both a lot, although they can wreak havoc in classes (hence they aren't in them). Both are bright and we have some very interesting exchanges. I pop in today on my walkabout. They are concerned; there is a rumour I might be leaving (this rumour has circulated since day one). I tease them. 'Yes, but you might get a new head who lets you use your phones and has fewer rules.'

Dawn looks thoughtful. 'Yeah, but miss, we're used to your rules now. They're clear. We don't want them to change.' I am tempted to ask them why, if that's the case, they both break them so regularly, but instead I read the essays they are writing.

FRIDAY 21 DECEMBER 2018

The last day of term; the mood in school is uncharacteristically sombre. One of our very supportive parents is an Anglican minister; I ask her if she will come into school and lead a prayer session, which she does, striking in her bright blue heels under her clerical garb. Attendance is voluntary, but the staff room is packed, silent, as she makes the point that regardless of faith or lack of it, we are all united in our thoughts for Pete and she asks Jesus to deliver the best outcome for our beloved colleague.

MONDAY 21 JANUARY 2019

I receive a voicemail message from Pete's sister. Things are getting worse. The message says she has been there all night and that there is nothing further they can do, they are just making Pete comfortable. She ends with, 'Sorry to have disturbed you, I know how busy you are.' The day takes on a strange air. BBC Radio call asking for an interview on whatever the new year's latest school issue is, but I don't even call them back. Sean leaves school early to go to the hospital.

TUESDAY 22 JANUARY 2019

7.40 p.m. I am in the shower and don't get to my phone, so Pete's sister has to leave me a message, which again begins, 'Sorry to trouble you,' and goes on to tell me that Pete has passed away at five o'clock this evening, very peacefully in his sleep. She tells me how much she and Pete's two brothers have appreciated the calls and help. I call her straight back. I utter the words of condolence and sadness that always, in these circumstances, seem so pointless but are what must be said. Then I call Jeff. Then I sit and for thirty minutes weep uncontrollably.

WEDNESDAY 23 JANUARY 2019

It is the hardest staff briefing I have ever had to give. I stand and read. I cannot look at the faces of my distraught staff for fear I will break down, and they need me today to be strong.

I have to bring to you the very sad news that many of you may well be aware of – Pete has died.

He suffered a mild seizure mid-December, and then a second, very serious one three days later. In hospital he received the very best care possible. However, life support was gradually withdrawn throughout the day on Monday and in the early evening of yesterday, he slipped away peacefully in his sleep. Throughout, he was supported by friends and family who loved him, and in this room none more so than Sean, who has been the best friend a man or woman could dream of.

We always stand together in our school – and now we

stand together in our grief. I am, as you are, upset, devastated, angry – but mostly sad. I am trying, as will you, to find comfort in knowing Pete is now at peace, and that any future that kept him trapped in a weak body, or robbed him of his faculties and his astonishing, scientifically brilliant mind, would have been a wicked one.

I liked, respected and cared for him deeply; *many* of you were close to him. Even those who weren't especially will feel the hole, the pain and the sadness of losing one of Team Lunsford. The children will feel it acutely. We must try, as much as we can, to be strong for them.

I have been in contact with some of you last night and thank you to all of you for your support and strength. The show must, and will, go on. We will be telling the pupils this morning in assemblies, and parents will be emailed a letter from myself, and we are also liaising with the local authority to secure hands-on, expert psychological support for pupils and staff who might need it.

Sean has put together something for pupils, which he will read to them; I will be by his side. It is beautiful, poignant, tender and practical.

I am in close contact with Pete's sister, and at some stage she will be coming in to school. She would like to meet Pete's friends and colleagues. I will of course keep you up to speed with any funeral arrangements. What we as a school community will be doing is of huge importance to honour Pete. There will be a voluntary memorial service here in school and we will be creating a memorial garden in his memory.

Ralph Waldo Emerson said, 'It is not the length of life, but the depth of life.' Pete's life has affected many people deeply. He will leave his mark. Pete had a complicated life; many do. What I do know is that this, here, us, you – we were a big and special part of his life. He told Sean numerous times that it was coming to this school, to teach science – a subject about which he was passionate – that got him through the day. Working with the pupils was a medicine for him that did him more good than anything a doctor could prescribe.

And later, in a hall full of weeping students, I tell them, 'March on. Mr Goddard cared desperately about you. All of you. The single best way you can honour his memory is to succeed. So work, work for yourselves, work for him, make him proud.'

WEDNESDAY 30 JANUARY 2019

I go with a young English teacher on a trip she has arranged through Women of the Future. Many of these girls have not been into the city centre. Nobody in their family has been to university, none of their parents have careers (many are not even in jobs). Raising their aspirations is as important a part of our mission as raising their exam results. Successful women from John Lewis talk to them about their careers and how they got there. The girls are timid but curious, polite but scared, but as the day progresses their excitement is palpable. The lift that whisks us silently up thirty-two floors to the Jo Malone foyer where they are met is the most thrilling ride of some of their young lives. They've written letters describing what they would get out of such a trip if chosen to attend. The letters are in my bag and their words rest in my heart.

> I am set on a career in law. I want to impress the people we may meet, so I will be presenting the best version of myself on the trip.

Or another:

> This trip would be amazing for me to see first-hand successful women in prestigious positions of authority. I feel very strongly that women shouldn't be held back by our gender. In fact, we should embrace it and challenge all aspects of toxic masculinity. I want schools to teach students that 'feminism' isn't a dirty word, that in fact we are all feminists if we believe that women and men should have equal rights.

And this:

> I find the many career choices in the world rather daunting, so I plan to use every lesson I learn on the trip as the tools to build myself that future I believe I deserve, as a hardworking young woman.

FRIDAY 1 FEBRUARY 2019

Vanessa is a complex character. She looks well looked after, can be polite and sweet, and is very bright. She can also be hideously confrontational, rude, violent and is operating more and more frequently out of our control. I know she has repeatedly run away from home and her mum is at her wits' end.

Steph emails me:

As I took over the Isolation room at the end of lesson 4, I asked Vanessa to sit down and be quiet. She did neither. I told all the other students to ignore her and not respond to her childishness. Vanessa responded by saying, 'I am a fucking child and I will speak to whoever the fuck I want.' When I asked another student to stop leaning back on his chair, Vanessa immediately started to swing on her chair. When I asked her to sit properly, she said, 'I will sit how the fuck I like. This school is always fucking telling me what to do.' I again politely asked her to be quiet at which she screamed, 'Fuck off, you are irrelevant, just like every fucking person in this stupid fucking school.' At this point you came in and as you know, the torrent continued.

I call her mum, a pleasant enough woman who clearly has zero control over her daughter at home. I note that Vanesa speaks to her mum like she speaks to us. Mum says, 'I am so sorry. And I'm surprised, as we went forest bathing last night, I thought today things might be better. Have you tried meditating with her? Can you maybe find her a safe place to read her affirmation?'

'Well, no,' I admit. 'No, because at the moment she's wandering the school.'

'Do read her the affirmation. We wrote it down so that when she goes into one she can read it and it will calm her down.'

I point out that, at this moment, that too is unlikely.

TUESDAY 5 FEBRUARY 2019

It is a gloriously hot day, unseasonal; the sun beats down as the mourners drive into the crematorium. Most of the sixth form have turned out; the girls are crying, the boys red-eyed. Many staff are attending. I had told staff that anyone who wished to go should do so, but we have still managed to keep the school open for three full year groups. As hard as it is for those of us here, it undoubtedly is going to be equally hard for those staff holding it together back at school.

We hear warm, wonderful memories from school friends, Pete's sister, an ex-colleague; we learn more about someone who was maverick, troubled, important, brilliant. His three children sit weeping; they later make the most heart-wrenching speech, standing side by side, gripping each other. Daniella, his 25-year-old daughter, tells the hushed congregation how hearing about the difference her dad made to the lives of others as a teacher had made her so happy. Luke and Abdul sit with heads hung low, shoulders shaking. Then it's my turn:

I feel blessed that we had Pete with us in our academy, albeit for a tragically short time. My memories of him are so vivid, I still can't believe he has gone. I think of his voice, that distinguished, distinctive voice, which resonated down the science corridor. I loved being in his lessons, and I went into them often. His A level physics class was one of very few lessons in this school where I honestly didn't have a clue what he was talking about. I loved observing his lessons, where he was *always teaching*; I rarely saw him sat down. Always at the board, pen in hand, explaining, unlocking – I could almost hear the click of understanding as pennies dropped. He was in that elite group of teachers, led by Mr Bryant and Mr Simmonds, who taught with one hand permanently in his trouser pocket, an act of casualness that told of the absolute ease with which science came to him, with which *teaching* came to him.

Headship brings a certain distance, a perhaps inevitable formality to relationships with staff. I didn't go down the pub with Mr Goddard (although I remember being very impressed with his ice-skating skills at one end-of-term event). I didn't know much about what he did at weekends or in the holidays. We did, however, often chuckle together at the fact that, by being the same age – only two months separate us – together we were helping to significantly raise the average age of the teachers in our school.

1966. It was a good year. A *great* year. I tell my staff I expect us to love our children. I do – and I love my staff too. I loved and cared for and respected Pete enormously. He was too young, too brilliant, too special to go, too early. I miss him. You miss him. I will never forget him. His star shines on.

WEDNESDAY 6 MARCH 2019

Olivia and Charles deliver the Oxbridge assembly. Their two ages added together only just equal mine, I realise with a shudder, but I don't care (much); I care about and adore their passion, their intellect, their determination to do yet another thing on top of all the wonderful things they do every day.

They loved their studies (Charles history at Cambridge, Olivia classics at Oxford) and they are genuinely evangelical about their desire to get our children to peep into the world of university, to capture their interest, to inspire them to aim high. Olivia talks animatedly about the extra-curricular things she took part in: the choir, the rugby. Charles talks about his love of history and how he got to talk and read about that for four years. The children are enchanted, genuinely interested. 'Who wants to go to university?' I ask. At least half of the room put their hands up (shoot them up, in fact) and I am reminded of the meeting with the Year 10 girls three years ago whose career aspirations started and ended with the nail bar or the tanning salon.

'What might you want to read?' asks Charles in his gentle, kind and yet (for one so young) compellingly authoritative voice, and we hear of aspiring linguists, authors, doctors, teachers.

I ask one young girl. 'Hair and beauty,' she beams. Much work still to do, but inroads made.

FRIDAY 8 MARCH 2019

Courtney and Dawn are discussing dinner. Or rather, Grant is discussing how every evening he, his wife and their young son have dinner, home-cooked, often by him; they eat it together, at a table, and talk. No phones. The girls look incredulous – look, in fact, genuinely puzzled, as if they don't understand what he's just said. I join in, tell them how I love to cook, how sitting round a dinner table and chatting is one of life's rich pleasures, how I too like my phone and find it useful but how there's no place for it ever around a meal table. I ask them cautiously what dinner's like in their house. Dawn shrugs. 'Mum cooks. Then she eats as she watches telly. I take it up to me room. Eat it off me lap, on me bed watching Netflix.'

TUESDAY 2 APRIL 2019

I listen to the news on the latest stabbing in the local area. Another young life tragically wiped out through this sickening increase in knife violence. A local community worker speaks about the breakdown in essential services, blames austerity, blames Early Help, criticises the police, of course blames the schools that have permanently excluded the victim. Absolutely no mention of family responsibility or liability. No talk of what parents should be doing to educate their own children, by not letting them out at all hours to roam the streets, spending more time with their children and less time on their phones, taking on the role of an actual parent rather than that of a friend. Enforcing home rules. No mention of that. None. Zilch.

SATURDAY 4 MAY 2019

I finish my open letter to applicants for the teaching vacancies we have. I need to do something different, it needs to stand out, the recruitment crisis is so chronic. But as John F. Kennedy said, 'When written in Chinese, the word "crisis" is composed of two characters. One represents danger; the other represents opportunity.'

Dear applicant,

Thank you for showing an interest in (maybe) joining our academy. We opened nearly three years ago as a new academy and are very proud of the success we have had to date. Our results have increased year on year – although there is still much to do – but some things have remained unchanged since day one: our insistence on high standards, our strict approach to discipline, our sky-high expectations for what our children can achieve and our determination to raise the aspirations and improve the life chances of every pupil. Our numbers are increasing, our parents write appreciative, positive emails to me (which far, far outnumber the odd few who complain about our high standards), and 100 per cent of my staff in our survey say they know what we are trying to achieve and enjoy their work. (Oh, and OFSTED gave us 'Good' across the board in our first inspection, but that is last in our list of proud achievements.)

I love our school, my staff and our children, and I love coming to work every day. I want you to do the same, and if you don't, you are in the wrong job or maybe just the wrong school. Teaching is a joyous, wonderful profession and a privileged one, giving us the opportunity to mould young lives and to transform life chances – I know that you remember your great teachers. But there is a teacher recruitment crisis out there, and if you are a hard-working, committed and talented teacher, you can – and should – be choosy. There are lots of schools and lots of jobs – why would you join us?

I look for only three things in my teachers: that you love children; that you are conscientious, committed and with a clear moral purpose; and that you are passionate and highly knowledgeable about your subject. If you are these things, I would love to meet you. In return, we don't preach work–life balance; we practise it. We have a no-marking policy, which means teachers don't spend hours unnecessarily marking (they don't mark!) but instead they use their time to plan exciting lessons, to discuss the best way to teach a topic, and to read books. We don't have unnecessary meetings (we have hardly any meetings) and we do no unnecessary paperwork – indeed, we have hardly any paperwork. We finish at two o'clock on a Friday, and I actively encourage staff to leave school at a sensible time every day – I don't care whose car is last in the car park and it isn't ever mine! Our email policy prohibits evening or weekend communication, and I expect teachers to enjoy and to relish every minute of their well-earned thirteen weeks' holiday.

We don't do jargon, we don't do clichés and we put common sense at the front of everything we do. I am constantly looking at school life to make sure we don't do anything that is unnecessary, and that all time is time well spent. We don't start (and then abandon) endless pointless initiatives, and I welcome the thoughts and suggestions of every member of the staff team; no one person has a monopoly on good ideas. Staff are supported by a highly visible and talented leadership team, excellent line management and a clear and enforced behaviour policy. I often describe myself as the conductor of the orchestra and I am privileged to lead an exceptionally talented, committed and wonderful team of teachers and support staff, who tell me that they enjoy their jobs and are proud to work in our school. If you would like to join them and me, and to continue our mission to make our good school great, please come and look around and see what I am describing in action. Feel free to email me directly to arrange this.

Postscript: It had barely gone live on the website when this pinged into my inbox:

Good evening, I am very interested in coming in and looking around your school and would relish the opportunity to meet the maths team. I have never read a Principal's welcome letter which has resonated with me so much. If you could email me with possible times and dates I would be very grateful.

THURSDAY 9 MAY 2019
Email from a parent:

Thank you from the bottom of my heart for giving Tony the chance to really come out of himself and succeed. I've had kids in a lot of different schools over the past fifteen years (I have four children and my eldest is twenty-two), but Lunsford is the most caring and supportive by a country mile. His educational and, more importantly, his emotional needs have been met and then some. He has become a very happy and well-rounded young man.

TUESDAY 14 MAY 2019

I have an angry parent meeting, in that the parent is super-angry and I am yet again resigned to hearing a lot of self-delusion from her about the ongoing poor behaviour of her sons. It is a strange meeting; she frequently tells me that God watches me and knows what I am doing, and that he is angry at me. I repeatedly catalogue the (long) list of rude, de-fiant, disruptive behaviour displayed by her children and ask her what she does at home to sanction them. Anticipating a difficult meeting, and knowing she is a churchgoer, I have garnered support by way of a governor who is a minister; his quiet, sensible manner manages to calm her and, in a bizarre twist, results in her shaking my hand as we end the meeting and telling me God is now in fact happy with me and approves of my rules. That evening I email John to thank him for his input. He replies, 'You are welcome, you know you have mine and God's full support! I don't know how you manage to stay so calm when parents get so angry.' And he signs off, in a rather unminister-like way, 'Anyway, I am off for a large whisky now. I know alcohol isn't the answer, but I've forgotten the question!'

TUESDAY 21 MAY

The press have got hold of an interview I have given in sup-port of schools taking a tough stance against abusive parents. As is so often the way, a twist is put that I am being driven out of Lunsford (after five years I have decided it is time to pass the baton on to new leadership, new eyes, new ideas) by the stroppy parents. The phone rings incessantly with requests for interviews (again I am rather surprised; schools acting like banks, shops, the NHS and all other public services in not allowing aggressive behaviour hardly seems newsworthy). As a lifelong fan, the one I most happily accept is finally to go on LBC with Iain Dale.

Being in the studio is a real thrill to someone who has listened to the show for so long, but the excitement soon wanes as we talk about schools, education, parents, leadership. A number of callers make for interesting dialogue, including a teacher bemoaning how long they spend working at home; I advise them, as always, to find another school. Then Iain says, 'Our final call is from Helen, who is in Lunsford!' My heart pounds. It may well be one of our angry parents, our critics, a Local; while I am always ready to defend our school, it is not how I want the show to end. But it is a current student. She starts by thanking me. She talks about her own time in the school and being in its predecessor. She speaks with simplicity and gratitude and hope. She talks with warmth about her teachers, she tells of her ambition to go to university and become a doctor. I am overwhelmed by emotion; this is what it's all about, this is why we have done what we do, and continue, every day, despite and against the critics and the naysayers and the angry, so that young people like Helen can thrive, will love school, will enjoy learning, and will go on to higher education. I manage to mutter a few words of thanks; the show ends and I cry all the way home.

My sister-in-law messages me: 'I heard the show, it was great. But how much did you pay Helen to call in?'

FRIDAY 24 MAY 2019

Some of our Year 12 design pupils are applying for work experience placements at a top-level architecture firm. Their eloquence and ambition really touch me. One pupil talks about how he wants to address the crisis around safe human habitation for those people who will be displaced as a result of global warming, another about how she wants to design smart buildings that use technology to adapt to what's happening outside and enable people inside to be more comfortable and more efficient – a job that didn't even exist when I was at school.

'I've realised that I didn't want an easy path and I want to be challenged every day. I want to be one of the people who help solve the energy problems in the world today and not create more, as I believe this is one of the most pressing issues society faces.'

'I believe architecture and engineering go hand in hand more today than ever. I believe buildings should be clever. They should work towards solving the climate crisis. To that end, I have a keen interest in passive buildings that have no carbon footprint.'

'I have moved countries frequently which enabled me to learn four languages and I am now learning signing. I am sometimes asked by the school to assist with non-English-speaking parents and students with translation. It feels great to be able to assist people as they navigate their way through unfamiliar territory and help them feel as comfortable and understood as if they were in their own home. I want to apply those same skills to designing houses, buildings and infrastructure that make people feel like they belong.'

The youth of today, huh?

FRIDAY 21 JUNE 2019

Reading the staff survey is the best birthday present I could have:

'Thanks for taking the time to listen to staff feedback – it means a great deal to be led by someone who wants to hear what we have to say and actually responds.'

'I just wanted to say thank you for believing in me and giving me a fantastic opportunity to be part of the academy. You have no idea how much it means to me that you listened. Always truly grateful.'

'I have loved being here and am thankful for (almost!) every moment. Your belief in me has helped me develop my own convictions more deeply and cemented my desire to stay in teaching permanently.'

TUESDAY 16 JULY 2019

Email from a new and neighbourly head of a nearby school that's due to open in two months:

After a very long year, it was energising to get the chance to visit your school yesterday, and I left feeling inspired and refreshed, unusual in July! The behaviour of your students was extremely impressive, as was the positivity and enthusiasm of your staff. I had a chance to talk to quite a few; they were full of praise about your leadership and spoke repeatedly about how you make them feel valued. One young teacher told me she was grateful for being part of the amazing team that has been created under your headship. What I got a sense of above everything else was a feeling of togetherness, a collective drive to do the right thing for the kids, and this permeates through the school. I have lots of brilliant ideas from your school and I am excited about putting them into practice in my own school in September.

WEDNESDAY 17 JULY 2019

Martina's mum rings me back an hour or so after my leaving her a message. She works as a doctor's receptionist and can't always answer the phone, which we ring a lot owing to her daughter's ongoing poor behaviour. As ever, she rushes over in her lunch hour. I tell her this is really Martina's last chance; she may have had a few of them, but I like mum, I like Martina, and when she is not being aggressive and rude, she can be delightful. A supportive parent gets more chances. We need to work together.

But today there is more on her mind than just reading Martina another riot act. 'I've kicked him out!' She looks delighted, and I think she wants me to be too.

'Well, Mrs Jones, I hope you're OK. You know your husband never liked anything we did, but divorce is tough.'

I am conscious of Martina, who is now quietly crying. Steph takes her next door for a tissue and the hug the younger teachers are convinced we are not allowed to give any more.

'So, last night as I got home a woman comes up to me on my own front doorstep. Said she'd met that bastard in a singles' bar. A singles' bar! Wanker! Said she didn't know he was married. She had loads of printouts of emails from him to her, saying how much he loved her and all the rest. I actually felt sorry for her. She had been lied to as much as I had. She said she'd chucked him when she found out, said she was so sorry, she was crying. I told her not to be sorry, told her it was the best thing she could have done for me. Now that I know, that wanker is never setting foot in my home again.' She beams at me, then looks rueful. 'But it's obviously upsetting for Martina. She heard me tell him last night to sling his hook.'

I know Martina has just got herself another lifeline.

MONDAY 22 JULY 2019

I read the reference for Steven, our Oxbridge hopeful, written by David, who himself went to Cambridge from a council estate upbringing:

Steven is a boy whom the rest of the Year 13 student body at Lunsford Academy, and indeed many of our younger students across the entire school, look to as a role model. He is also a dedicated, enthusiastic, curious and very able student, achieving the highest GCSE results in his year. These achievements are all the more impressive given that Steven and his peers spent the first portion of their secondary careers in a failing school, which was subsequently closed by the Department for Education. This school reopened as The

Lunsford Academy in September 2014. The school is for pupils aged 11–18 and takes students from some of the most deprived wards in the country. The predecessor school was characterised by inadequate teaching, poor behaviour, low expectations and an appalling reputation. During the transition period, Steven's peers experienced significant change and he now faces the additional challenge of being in the first group to undertake Year 13 study. He is a white working-class boy and would be the first member of his family to ever attend university. I have no reservations in recommending him as a first-class candidate for the study of English literature at your university.

FRIDAY 26 JULY 2019

Gavin bounds into my office. I would say he almost skips. Almost. 'Miss, we got the maths results back, only one person in the class got a 5 – me!' He is beaming.

'That is brilliant, well done,' and I hold out my hand, which he shakes with a mixture of teenage embarrassment and visible pride. 'Your dad will be really happy. This means that an 8 or 9 is in our grasp, yes?'

He says nothing, just nods (still beaming) and saunters out. Sometimes I really love my job.

AN OPEN LETTER TO THE SECRETARY OF STATE FOR EDUCATION

Dear Secretary of State,

Please forgive the lack of personalisation, but the person doing your job changes very regularly, and I fear that this letter will be applicable for some time yet. So, I've opted for generic but accurate over polite.

Firstly, a reminder: that all those of us who work in education are lucky. We are privileged. We carry a unique and special responsibility. Arguably, you hold the most important role of all. You control education. You are in charge of education. It's an easy job to be quite rightly proud about. It's an easy job to talk movingly and passionately about, in the set-piece speeches, in the news reports, in the interviews. It's easy for any ambitious politician to talk about the significance and importance of education, to reference the moulding of young minds and future lives, to create touching sound bites about their own school days and memorable teachers. It is easy to make it sound wonderful and exciting, to offer a list of promises and commitments, to describe how you will really make a difference to future generations. Who wouldn't want to run that world?

And after all – we are *all* experts on education. We all went to school, didn't we? And we all know how it can be better. But here's the irony: you aren't an expert. Having been to school does not make you an expert in education leadership, just as being ill does not equip you to run a hospital, nor does being arrested mean you could lead the police. You're running the most important department in the whole of government, and you really need to listen to us, the people who do run good schools, who actually *do* mould lives and transform life chances. Because unless you have run the complex, frustrating, challenging, rewarding, uplifting, precious and special organisation that is a school, trust me, you really don't know what schools need.

I have worked in schools for almost thirty years, mostly in inner cities and in so-called challenging schools. I have worked in three schools that were in special measures when I joined and which we healed. I love my work. I think teaching is the finest, the noblest, the most rewarding job you can do. Of course, I am biased, but there is no more important job than this. There are other important jobs. Jobs that impact massively on other people's lives. Nurse. Artist. Midwife. Police officer. Chef. Secretary. Ambulance driver. Running a business. Running a home. But I remain unashamedly dewy-eyed about our job. Teachers are society's most valuable asset. Teaching is, it truly is, the most joyous of professions, the most incredible of honours, the best, most fun, most rewarding, most demanding, most varied and the most, most, most important of jobs that anyone could do (or up there with doctors and surgeons since they save lives, I suppose, but then, in many ways, we teachers do that too, often, and for far less cash and certainly less recognition).

Schools are special places. The Germans have a word that doesn't translate – 'bildung', which means the complete moral, emotional, intellectual and civic development of a person. That is what school is about, and you should be viewing education as consisting of far more than things that can be easily measured. You should be seeing our schools as places where the older generation passes on knowledge, develops skills, and deliberately cultivates the values and attributes that the next generation will need. What a responsibility you and we hold, and what a privilege.

I'm as passionate today as I was when I started out as a teacher, if hopefully a little bit more clued up. But the things I believed then I still believe now, as a successful head teacher. My principles and core views have never changed. I'm so proud of being a teacher and I love being a head, despite working in the most challenging of communities. But education has become over-complicated. The profession needs educated, eloquent, clever, inspiring people to be entering it in droves. We should be making that happen and not pandering to the unprofessional myth-maker teachers who would have the country believe that all classrooms are in chaos and teaching is miserable when it absolutely shouldn't be and doesn't have to be.

Because education is in crisis. Deep, deep crisis. There are not enough great teachers already in the system, and the supply line is broken at both ends: there are certainly nowhere near enough potentially great teachers considering entering it, and too many leaving prematurely. Don't throw statistics at me. Don't reference the increase in people going into teacher training. Get out of your bubble and enter my world, the one where an advert for a head of English yields no applications, the world where I am only ever one teacher away from yet another decline in a subject's exam results, and a corresponding increase in my inbox of angry parental emails about why did Mr X leave and what happened to Ms Y, who was so amazing, and how Toby/Chloe/Brad used to hate maths/physics/English before but now they want to go to university to study it. I have this conversation with every head I meet, and despite it being so serious it has become something of a joke. There are not enough teachers. There are not enough new recruits. The fragile world of education teeters on the brink. This is the reality for every single head in the country and the problem is just getting worse, every year.

And why is this?

Let's start with the f-word, or lack of it. Finances. Stop telling us how much extra money you've put into schools. The more important f-word is fact, and it is a fact that there is chronic underfunding in schools. Don't tell me there is more money going into schools than ever before; there isn't enough. And

I am not talking about profligacy or waste: trust me, over the years I have seen huge amounts of waste in the system and badly run schools, money frittered on pointless initiatives and useless consultants – no, I am not talking about those, I am talking about my school and thousands like it where budgets are restrained and finances are well run, where prudency and economy are lived, and where every single penny is respected as the public money that it is, and is spent wisely and well – but there just isn't enough of it.

Stop interfering with these institutions you claim to respect and undermining the school leaders you insist you listen to. I mean, who seriously thought it was a good idea to change the grading system? Nobody sane and normal really understands 'progress 8' and if exams were too easy, why didn't you just make them harder rather than changing the well-understood grading system of letters to ambiguous numbers? Is a 4 really a pass, like a 5 is, or is it just the equivalent of going to a poly in the '80s: everyone pretended it was the same as university, but everyone really knew it wasn't. The success of a school is in any case about so much more than its progress 8 score. I am quite sure that I will hear you say that schools are not just about exams, but if you truly believe that, why the constant reference to and high pro-file of the league tables? Why not be radical and abolish them? Of course schools are about students gaining qualifications, of course a great school wants every child to be stretched and challenged and to fulfil every ounce of their potential and (if appropriate; it isn't for everyone) to go off to the best universities, but why not talk more about – maybe a league table for?! – all those other hugely important things that pulse at the heart of great schools: joy and happiness, laughter, excitement, curiosity, mutual respect and manners and smiles, and all the many, many things that create lifelong memories for children way more important than the school's ranking in the *Daily Mail*?

And please – stop banging on about the red herring that is the grammar school system. Stop misusing language: stop talking about discipline, ethos and high standards when you talk about grammar schools, as if these are the sole preserve of the selective schools – they aren't. Please recognise that these are words that should be used to describe every school in the country. This country doesn't need any more selection. It just needs every school to be a great school. That's it. Nothing more or less. Simple. Children to walk to their nearest school, with their friends and siblings, not having to worry about tutoring or first choices, just walking to the closest school, secure in the knowledge that it is a great one, that they will be stretched and challenged, encouraged and supported, nurtured and nourished. Spend less time trying to argue the unarguable nonsense that is selection aged ten, and more time on getting rid of bad heads and making every school fabulous.

I try constantly to dispel the myths, but this should in fact be your job. Your job should be trying to get the most well-educated, the most well-read, the most inspiring into our schools. There is a myth about pay – pay is not bad. You don't go into education to make millions, but I don't know of many teachers who don't have nice lifestyles and lots of travel. We don't apologise for our thirteen weeks' holiday; in fact, we are (or we should be) rather smug about it. It is our perk, like a company car or an expense account, and we should enjoy every day of it (even if it is annoying that the fares rocket during school holidays).

Dispel all the myths: excessive paperwork, hours of marking, unruly classrooms – these are trademarks of failing institutions, where leadership is poor, and have no place in successful, vibrant, well-run schools, regardless of area or circumstance. Invest in alternative education. Schools like mine deal every day with the disadvantaged, the neglected, the angry and the abused. Schools do incredible, miraculous work, they keep children safe when their families don't, they nurture and nourish and care for the unloved. But they are at breaking point. There need to be thousands more alternative providers to teach and help these troubled youngsters. There need to be thousands more bright, well-qualified, committed people being attracted to teaching and staying in it, and there simply aren't, and this is your job, your most important challenge and one I urge you to take on.

The future of our country depends on educating our youth. It depends on having excellent, well-run, well-equipped schools, where brain and character are developed equally. It depends on schools where aspiration is sky-high, technology and the arts are loved equally, and sport, music, drama and dance are thriving. It depends, ultimately, on having a teaching profession that attracts the brightest and the best, attracts them in their thousands, and makes being a teacher the most lauded, respected, admired and revered job in the world. Because it is certainly the best one.

POSTSCRIPT: SUMMER 2020

'We do not have to become heroes overnight. Just a step at a time, meeting each thing that comes up, seeing it as not as dreadful as it appeared, discovering we have the strength to stare it down.'
– ELEANOR ROOSEVELT

'There are decades where nothing happens, and there are weeks when decades happen.'
– VLADIMIR LENIN

I had moved on from Lunsford to lead an international school in Spain and, almost overnight, we are all plunged into a strange new norm. As well as the usual restrictions placed on me, as on everyone – over family, socialising, travel – running a school remotely becomes the biggest challenge of my professional life to date. As a teacher, I have reflected hard on what this period (for, as I write, we are still locked in it) has taught me, as well as what I have learnt, as a human being and as a leader, and what I have tried to teach my children (and staff) alongside the curriculum.

WEEK 1

Teachers have become once again the heroes of the piece – at first. In my school, seeing what was looming on the track ahead, we have barely a handful of days for teachers and children to upskill themselves with the technological know-how required for online live teaching and learning. For that is what we now provide – from day one, full live learning for all students. The same timetable. The same timings. The same teachers. Teachers sitting in their kitchens and their bedrooms, their lives on display behind them but their minds fully focused on delivering fantastic live lessons. We know that to many children, their teacher is so much more than the person who gifts them knowledge. Their teacher is someone they look to, look up to, who they learn more from than just their timetabled subject. In these strange times, they miss being with their teachers (and we miss being with all of them), so we want to do the next best thing and let them see our faces and hear our voices. We are all committed to ensuring that our children's learning will not suffer. We advise parents on the importance of keeping to a routine: parents tell me they are keeping up the school rules; some even tell me that they get their children to wear their school uniform.

WEEK 2

Rather like a snow day, at first not being in school inevitably carries a frisson of excitement for some children. But very quickly the reality sets in for them, not least because school is a place of fun and socialising as well as learning. Knowing that we are feeling worried, scared, uncertain, I urge my staff to remember that our children are feeling these things just as acutely and, with the innocence and natural anxiety of child-hood, probably more so. My staff work flat out to ensure excellent lessons. I hear more every day about the potential of e-learning and countless stories of brilliant e-lessons and excellent work being done remotely by our children. We publicly promote, every day, particularly commendable efforts by our young people.

When I was a child, there were three channels on the television. I can remember when 'Breakfast Television' started, to a great fanfare; prior to that there weren't any programmes on TV before about 11 a.m. There were only landline phones, and if we went out, we would have a ten pence piece for emergencies for a pay phone. I can vaguely remember one computer in my school in my final year in sixth form. People used typewriters. We all went to libraries to borrow real books. Holidays (if we were lucky enough to go on one) were booked in a high street travel agent. Technology (which has already revolutionised our lives: impossible to think of no mobile phones, or smart TVs, or Netflix, or social media) has, in these difficult times, become our lifeline.

WEEK 3

Long hours locked inside lead us all to reflect. Life is usually so hectic, complicated, rushed. We don't have enough time for the things and people that matter, we never feel we have done our to-do list. So many people never feel satisfied. This virus has forced us to slow down. We can't go out. We can't see loved ones. We can't socialise. We are trapped. I am absolutely determined to stay positive, to count my blessings. I am determined not to waste away hours on the internet. I am going to do all those simple things I have promised myself for so long, for years, but have always been far 'too busy' to achieve. I am going to spend time away from any screen. I am going to read more. I am going to learn more from that reading. I am going to reflect on things more fully. I am going *to be*. And I am going to feel appreciative.

The purpose of life is not to get everything done, I tell my staff in my weekly e-briefing, and as we tick things off our to-do list, new things replace them. There is more to life than increasing its speed. All the time we are fixated on getting things done, we will never get a sense of calm and wellbeing. In reality, (almost) everything can wait. The global spiritual leader Thich Nhat Hanh says, 'We have a tendency to think in terms of doing and not in terms of being. We think that when we are not doing anything, we are wasting our time. But that is not true. Our time is first of all for us to be. To be what? To be alive, to be peaceful, to be joyful, to be loving. That is what the world needs most.'

WEEK 4

Within a month, the life we enjoyed, with its freedoms and frivolities, has been replaced by something we could barely have imagined. We have new phrases that only weeks ago were unheard of, and now we pepper our every conversation with them – self-isolating, social distancing, lockdown. In what I now realise was the last meal out I was to have for quite a while, I think back to a conversation I had just over a month ago with the waiter about the unravelling situation. He was young, friendly and enthusiastic. 'I think this is going to bring out the best in people and the worst in people!' he said to me, thoughtfully. I believe he is right. For all the stories we originally heard of people selfishly stockpiling goods they don't need, we hear of supermarket CEOs declaring times when only the vulnerable will be able to shop. For all the ugly scenes of shoppers brawling over toilet rolls – over toilet rolls, for goodness sake! – we hear of communities galvanising the younger members to look out for the elderly and the lonely. People are urged to put postcards through letter boxes of vulnerable neighbours offering help; people rally to help those living alone and use social media to unite them with those who can provide assistance.

The kindness of people, at all times and of all ages, never ceases to inspire me. Even while we are all struggling, we still continue to teach our children other important values and principles. In our e-assemblies we talk to the children about kindness, and encourage them, despite the *very* real constraints currently upon us, to practise random acts of kindness; if ever there was a time when we need to promote kindness, it is surely now. We emphasise to our children the importance of appreciation. So tempting in these challenging times to feel sorry for ourselves; we urge them, now more than ever, to count their blessings. We encourage them to be appreciative of what we have, and always, always look to those who have less. The role of a school as a moral compass and instiller of values has never been more important.

WEEK 5

The comedian Ricky Gervais said in one of his stand-up shows that humour can be 'a sword, a shield and a medicine'. At the start of the pandemic, the internet was awash with jokes. Mostly they revolved around all-day drinking and weight gain – fattening the curve. With the increase in adults working from home and using video conferencing, people seemed initially to spend more time studying the homes of their colleagues and bosses than focusing on the discussion. People were let into each other's homes, into their studies, their kitchens, their gardens. People fixated on the details these glimpses reveal – their bookshelves, their wine racks, their decor. One vexed home worker said that while he will get over the virus, he will never get over his colleague's poor taste in books! But an increasing number of jokes are now about home schooling, of the stress it carries, and with it a palpable recognition of what teachers do, day in, day out.

Teachers as heroes. 'If the schools are closed for too long,' one joke goes, 'the parents are going to find a vaccine before the scientists!' The reality of parents having their children at home with them all day means a new respect and admiration emerges, which is welcomed. My teachers are being magnificent. In front of a screen all day, planning lessons all evening, assessing students' online work, calling home to check in with children (and parents), while in many cases also keeping their own families afloat, their own children sat at the kitchen table next to them doing their own e-learning. My teachers have their own worries, their own personal situations, their own family dramas, but they must put them to one side. As always, it is children first. The children who are slipping and sliding in these unstable times are hopefully feeling held by the security of their teachers. And at the end of each week, when a night out with friends or a gathering with family might ordinarily have beckoned and helped teachers make it through to that week's finishing line, such pleasures are, of course, still denied us all. My role as a leader has never felt more critical, and I have rarely felt more privileged or more humble. Through daily emails, Zoom calls and handwritten cards (which take weeks to be delivered), I keep up a constant stream of thanks and appreciation, of encouragement, a virtual acknowledgement of all that they are doing. In times of social distancing, connecting with my staff has never been more important.

WEEK 6

As the Easter holiday approaches, a time for many of renewal and hope, of forgiveness and new life, it is certainly a time right now of reflection. Before we were all forced to slow down, I reflect, so many of us were rushing through life and maybe forgetting to acknowledge and to show appreciation for the things that other people do to make our lives easier. I am increasingly, in these strange times, reflecting more and more on the people who help me. I come across this uplifting story:

Charles Plumb was a US Navy jet pilot and Vietnam veteran. After seventy-five combat missions, his plane was destroyed by a surface-to-air missile. Plumb ejected and parachuted into enemy hands; he was captured and spent six years in a communist Vietnamese prison. He survived the ordeal and went on to lecture on the lessons he learnt from that experience.

One day, when Plumb and his wife were sitting in a restaurant, a man at another table came up and said, 'You're Plumb! You flew jet fighters in Vietnam from the aircraft carrier *Kitty Hawk*. You were shot down!'

'How in the world did you know that?' asked Plumb.

'I packed your parachute,' the man replied.

Plumb gasped in surprise and gratitude. The man pumped his hand and said, 'I guess it worked!'

Plumb assured him, 'It sure did. If your 'chute hadn't worked, I wouldn't be here today.'

Plumb couldn't sleep that night, thinking about that man: 'I kept wondering what he had looked like in a Navy uniform: a white hat; a bib in the back; and bell-bottom trousers. I wonder how many times I might have seen him and not even said, "Good morning, how are you?" or anything, because I was a fighter pilot and he was just a sailor.' Plumb thought of the many hours the sailor had spent at a long wooden table in the bowels of the ship, carefully weaving the shrouds and folding the silks of each 'chute, holding in his hands, each time, the fate of someone he didn't know.

Plumb went on to give inspirational lessons to people. He would also point out that he needed many kinds of parachutes when his plane was shot down over enemy territory: he needed his physical parachute, his mental parachute, his emotional parachute and his spiritual parachute. He called on all these supports before reaching safety.

I tell this story to the children in an end-of-term e-assembly. Sometimes, I say to the camera, in the daily challenges that life gives us, especially now, we miss what is really important. We fail to say hello, please or thank you, to congratulate someone on something wonderful that has happened to them, pay a compliment, just do something nice for no reason. How many jobs go unnoticed and people unappreciated, people who work so hard and yet often get little recognition for their efforts? Who, I ask the sea of faces I can't see but who I know are listening, has been packing your parachute?

I reflect that night on who has played their part in packing mine – the supportive emails I have been sent, the personal anecdotes that have inspired me, the wonderful teaching that our children receive, the support of my team, the kindness of so many.

WEEK 7

Of course, not all schools are doing the incredible work that mine are. We know that too many youngsters are not getting good lessons. The most disadvantaged are yet again the ones who miss out the most. Gloomy predictions point to further years of the most vulnerable slipping behind academically. Teachers as heroes is now becoming teachers as villains – how quickly the tide turns. As talk turns to the reopening of schools, the unions do what they usually do: act in an unhelpful, divisive and aggressive way. The Children's Commissioner accuses them of 'unseemly squabbling' and not putting children first. The papers too turn against teachers, the journalists scathing – one of the most trusted professions yet again being told off and told what to do by one of the least trusted! Public opinion seems to turn against teachers too. We start to be accused of enjoying being off, enjoying lying in the gardens in the unusually good weather, of not providing work for children. LBC is full of experts; everyone knows what is best. I am reminded of a comment by Hillary Clinton: 'Everyone is entitled to his own opinion, but not his own facts.' Everyone knows when schools should open, and how. Schools, those most social of places, are told their children will need to practise social distancing but with scant detail on how that unlikeliest of tasks might be achieved when the same number of pupils still need to use the same amount of space. Criticism mounts of those feckless teachers and their long holidays. I don't recognise any of this as the norm. I know that everywhere teachers' resourcefulness and resilience have been triumphant, so many schools have quickly adapted to the 'new normal', providing everything from laptops to school meals to hope. I have never been more proud of my profession, as it demonstrates a determination that the children and young people in our care will come through this crisis as well as is humanly possible.

WEEK 8

Although our children are working hard and my teachers are flat out, I urge balance. I am hearing of children working excessively long days, of them putting additional stress on themselves, worrying about deadlines, of feeling overloaded. I remind our parents that while school *is* our children's norm, normal must also mean play, must mean downtime, must mean relaxation. They must have a break from their studies at break and lunchtime. They must end the school day at the normal time. The phone or the screen, so often the bane of our lives, becomes our new best friend; I ask parents to make sure their children use it to speak to their real best friends, to laugh, to share jokes, to talk to family members they may not be seeing for a while, but also to take a total break from technology. For those lucky enough to have a garden, I ask them to ensure their children play in it. If not, I encourage them to get their children to cook with them in the kitchen, help with chores, read with them, play with them, chat with them, laugh with them, comfort and reassure them. 'We will get through this,' I say, 'we will get through this together, and life will be normal again, one day, for us all.'

I am not sure I believe this.

WEEK 9

My leadership is being tested. I realise I haven't had a day off in seventy-two days. I had a Zoom call with my CEO on Easter Sunday and it didn't feel odd. Our parents are supportive but demanding, wanting different things, their own anxieties and stresses frequently transferred onto the school. I get around thirty-five emails a day that I sit down to respond to every evening, with a large G&T. So many parents are also working from home, resources are shared, tempers are short. Parents worry they can't give adequate support to their children. They want me to predict the future. At times their expectations and demands are crazily unrealistic. 'You never know how strong you are until being strong is your only choice' is written above my desk, but I don't feel strong. I am trying to find my own new normal, with the responsibility of leading my students and staff through their own uncertain times. I turn to an uplifting leadership book by Ariana Huffington. 'In times of crisis the need for leadership comes into sudden clear focus,' I read, as people crave strong leadership and clear communication. 'What is expected of leaders in times of crisis is not stamina, it is judgement, and that can only come from a place of inner strength and calm.'

I have never felt less calm.

WEEK 10

If my staff are magnificent, so too are our children. 'Resilience' is usually found on most schools' mission statements and held up as a quality children should develop, to help them to cope with all the bumps in the road. Of all the qualities our children are having to call upon – their inner strength, their compassion, their independence – there is certainly none being tested right now more than their resilience. Every day as we face yet more challenge, uncertainty, stress, anxiety, doubt, fear, confusion – our children are facing this too. They know we are in a global crisis. They know that things are uncertain, that their life has changed dramatically, that their parents are anxious, that they can't see in person their grandparents, their friends, their teachers. They see the news, they read the fake news, they are growing up, in many cases, far too soon.

And yet so many of our young people are striving away at their studies, giving it their best, trying their hardest. Our weekly newsletter showcases what they have been learning that week, brims with examples of exceptional work. Teachers talk of additional effort, of how our young people are helping others, showing kindness, showing humour. In these challenging times the grit, determination, character and resilience so many of our children are displaying every day humbles me. But as we applaud our children, we also encourage them, in e-assemblies, to think of other children all around the globe. Children now trapped in frightening households, without the oasis that is school. Children whose homes are blighted by neglect, abuse, poverty, loneliness, emptiness. Children who have none of the material comforts that so many of us enjoy.

WEEK 11

With the cancellation of public exams this summer, it seems that teachers are to be entrusted with the task of awarding grades. For many children, not sitting exams is not what they want. I know many of them feel robbed. However, I reassure them and their parents that, of all the challenges I have faced in my career, overseeing this process, going through every single grade that is awarded to every single student in every single subject will be done with the utmost integrity, rigour, detail and care. I am lucky: in my school I have not only great teachers but experienced and expert subject leaders. In lengthy Zoom meetings we walk through every single student's performance, in detail; I grill them on the evidence used to reach each grade, the accuracy in predicting past grades of individual teachers. I think sadly and with a shudder of those schools where students have had inconsistency of teaching, maybe been taught by a succession of supply staff, where teaching has been poor and subject leadership lacking. How the heads in those schools will be able to award grades with any degree of integrity, let alone confidence, is beyond me. Yet again, it is likely that the disadvantaged will suffer, their ability will have been hidden, their potential unreached, and the grades awarded will not be what they were capable of achieving, had they been in a good school. And when I deliver the end of Year 11 e-assembly, I tell the students that while they will for ever be the year that didn't sit exams,* were they ever to be mocked for that or indeed their qualifications questioned, they must stand tall and proudly counter that far from it: having had their grades awarded by teachers who knew them so well, and who had taught them for

---

* It was galling, for those of us silly enough still to listen to unkind commentators, to hear the doubt and cynicism about the exam results from so many. The least trusted of the professions – journalists and politicians – casting doubt on the integrity of one of the most trusted – teachers. Families hand their children to us when they wouldn't hand their wallet to a total stranger; they hand us their most precious possessions, entrust us to teach them, to inspire them, to care for them, to mentor and nurture them. But when it comes to assessing them – they distrust us!

years, in fact their grades were awarded with more evidence, more scrutiny and more reliability than ever before.

WEEK 12

Children have been out of school for three months. This sentence is being said so widely that its dark meaning is being diluted. For a quarter of a year, there has been no school for many, many children. Slowly, cautiously, some schools are starting to reopen, for some age groups. Classroom teaching resumes, albeit very differently to previously: later start, earlier finish, masks on in corridors, reduced curriculum, restricted play time. Of course, some middle-class families are choosing to keep their children at home. But these children, with their Zoom ballet lessons, their online piano and Japanese, their family mealtimes, their communal watching and discussing of the news, will not suffer. Families are being reassured by the Boden-clad Mumsnet brigade not to worry about home schooling: teach your children other things, bake with them, sing with them, teach them other life lessons, not geography or phonics. These children will come through this period relatively unscathed.

But the children who will suffer are, as ever, the poorest. They have been left behind, again, by a government that can build a hospital in nine days but cannot get its children back to school. By a country where many children will be allowed to go into Primark or the pub before they will be back in the classroom. The government makes lofty pronouncements that amount to nothing; they don't consult with school leaders but merely talk of how much money is being poured in, with no idea of how this might be used. They talk of catch-up that can't be staffed, of laptops that never materialise, of tutorials and help for 'the most disadvantaged' (a phrase so overused it loses all impact) that will never be provided. Disadvantaged children, whom it was hard enough to get into school and to get engaged at the best of times, will now fall even further behind their better-off peers. These are the children I used to teach, children who my friends in tough schools still tell me about. The fifteen-year-old girl who has submitted no online homework but who has given birth during lockdown. The Year 8 boy whose mother greeted the deputy head, when he did a home visit at three in the afternoon, still in her dressing gown, her son having not yet left his bedroom and his Xbox. The Year 10 girl who has not been heard of since lockdown began. For these youngsters, this will amount to a catastrophic and irretrievable loss of learning.

The gulf widens ever deeper between rich and poor, between private and state. Many schools, like mine, have staff working extremely hard to provide online lessons all day, every day. Some do not. The head who called out those 'tanned teachers' who have not been working hard (a tiny minority) becomes, inevitably, a hero with the public, whose envy of teacher holidays is never far from the surface. Social media is again in a frenzy over the lack of teaching and support from some teachers and some schools, an appalling neglect that is utterly indefensible but that is also not the norm. Many teachers have continued to go to work despite risks to their own health, have gone into schools through the holidays, have been working flat out to provide effective teaching. The lack of parental encouragement for many poorer children, the parents who will take their children to crowded beaches but won't send them to school – this makes for far fewer headlines and criticism than that directed at 'all these lazy teachers'. The experts on Twitter criticise and castigate and condemn all teachers, based, as ever, on scant evidence, just a desire to damn. It will take years for the teaching profession to regain the respect it deserves.

As I often do when feeling down from all the twits on Twitter who know everything about everything, I turn to the words and wisdom of Geoff Barton, the leader of ASCL, who writes to fellow school leaders:

> As I say so often, these things shall pass. My hunch remains that we will resurface to create an education system more certain of its values, more trusting of its people, and more determined to focus on the things that truly matter – indeed, perhaps especially those things not easily measurable but which have never seemed more important. Just as nature is currently reasserting itself, so, perhaps, is our inherent humanity.

AFTERWORD

The response to this book when it was published back in March 2022 was as humbling as being a school leader. It was written in the hope of promoting the joys of teaching, highlighting the privilege of leadership, encouraging teachers both to stay in and to join the profession, and celebrating countless children, young people, teachers and support staff. To receive emails from people I have never met, will never meet, describing the impact my words had made on them was profoundly moving. The head of a primary school who wrote that after a gruelling term when he'd taken the school from 'Inadequate' to 'Good', 'the stories shared and the reflections you presented were honest and refreshing and just what I needed to hear. I just wanted you to know what a difference it has made.' The early career teacher who told me my words had given him 'much food for thought and reassurance that an approach of sky-high expectations is the best way forward, perhaps most of all for those from disadvantaged backgrounds, and it has inspired me to continue making my own small contribution in challenging schools'. I have been inspired and encouraged by these hugely appreciated messages and reviews. I continue to love my job and think teaching is the most wonderful career – but it's not enough for just me to believe that. If we are to fix the crisis in education, new and existing teachers must be supported and encouraged to stay in the profession, and urgent action is needed across the system, not least from government.

To have had five Education Secretaries in a year would be funny were it not so desperately worrying; the rapid turnover of Prime Ministers only adds to the sense of uncertainty. When 90 per cent of schools in England expect to run out of money in the next year but the government responds by imposing spending cuts; when the Department for Education continually misses its own targets for teacher recruitment; when teachers see no option but to strike due to the continued refusal to invest in education, it is hard to see whose interests are served by the vacuum of leadership in our country.

Challenges in education have never been felt more keenly than in managing school life post-pandemic, with its dramatic impact on especially the most disadvantaged, whom it was hard enough to get into school before. The exam success of 2021/22's Year 13, who had their final GCSE year turned upside down by the pandemic and then a tumultuous return to school, was a remarkable testament both to them and to their teachers. Spiralling inflation, an unprecedented energy crisis and their effects on both families and school budgets have only exacerbated the difficulty. And yet as I write this, the current

PM, in keeping with the 'Westminster knows best' culture, has decreed that we need more maths, much more maths – when every school leader knows that recruiting enough maths teachers even for just the current situation is hard, recruiting great ones more so. Currently, one in eight of those who teach maths are not specialist maths teachers. Every subject in secondary schools is now deemed a shortage one, every initial teacher training target is being missed, and a quarter of teachers leave the profession after just two years (a third after five).

But despite all this, I remain optimistic, hopeful, positive – and that is because I've seen first-hand the passion, the ingenuity and the dedication of our best and brightest teachers, and I've seen the difference they can make to children's lives. If you are thinking of leaving teaching, think again: change school, not profession. Listen to the measured and reasonable political voices on education, not the scaremongers. Heed the wisdom and encouraging counsel of the ASCL's Geoff Barton, LBC's Iain Dale and England's school behaviour tsar Tom Bennett. Visit Michaela Community School and see the astonishing, life-changing work that the teachers do there day in, day out (and they don't mark, or take work home). Keep reading and learning about the fantastic work that goes on in so many other schools across the country, keep believing in common sense and keep maintaining high expectations, keep hoping that one day (soon) an ex-teacher will become Education Secretary, and keep remembering, every day, that you are changing lives.

ACKNOWLEDGEMENTS

I hope that many people read this book and I hope that many people recognise themselves in it. Those teachers changing lives. Those children showing resilience and spirit. Those school leaders ignoring the noise, showing bravery, dedication, determination.

I hope that those who helped us in our mission know the love, respect and appreciation I will for ever feel, and the life-long friendships I will cherish. I hope you can find yourselves among these pages and that this book brings back memories of a truly special and memorable period in our lives, especially Jeff, Steph Cresswell, David Jones, Claire, the VP, Charles and Sean.

For such a personable job, schools still tend to refer to staff through the impersonal style of initials, and so in that spirit I thank and salute all the many incredible teachers, leaders, governors, trustees and staff who helped, supported, encouraged and inspired me during really challenging times, and who left their fingerprints on our school and our students: to BTH, CDM, CFR, CHI, CMO, DCO, DOT, GCR, HEV, HSA, HSU, IDA, JCA, JEA, JFA, JFI, JLA, KST, KWI, LBU, NTA, PAT, PMA, PSW, RAP, RDI, RLE, SCU, SIN, SPO, TKN, TSU. To those not listed, apologies, there are just so many and I am getting on a bit.

I met many of my dearest friends in various schools going back for more years than I care to remember; thank you for being true friends. I have learnt so much from your own stories about how to run a school and how not to run one, and our friendships have often helped to keep me buoyant when waters got choppy. To Sallie (for easing my nerves with a friendly smile as I waited, terrified, to greet my first ever 'real' class nearly thirty years ago); to two of the best, most special teachers and people, Karin and Sally, thank you for making me laugh until I cry and for your warmth, wit and wisdom; to Patrick; to Pete (my friend and mentor, RIP, you changed so many lives); to Jeremy, Laura (in the mission that was out of control!); and laterally to Katharine, for giving me encouragement to stand firm and be brave.

Thanks go to the friends I have outside of teaching; you've always given me love, support and many much needed laughs: Liza, Paul and Chris (and Eloi Merle, France's best B&B!), Dave, Ian, Sonia, Chris and Cathy, Derek, Fiona and Lizzy, Nigel and Glynis, Laura and David, Michelle (across the years and the miles), and Susan and Alex, for creating in Son Arnau in Selva a perfect oasis of calm and beauty, and where many of these lines were penned.

To my parents: while sadly they cannot read this book, they helped to instil in me important values and a deep respect for education. To my family, who have always shown me love and encouragement: to John, Judy, Gemma, Phil, Hazel and, if I was lucky, Richard (and it means the world, by the way).

To the excellent team I work with at BIC SAP: you are a world-class orchestra, and one it is a privilege to conduct; thank you for the welcome you gave me two and a half years ago and the brilliant work you continue to do. The teaching in our school is truly outstanding, as is the nourishment and nurture you give on a daily basis to our students. Headship is about plate spinning and I thank the wonderful team I have around me who ensure we (most of the time) keep all those plates in the air, especially Alex, John, Janine, Lizzie, Lucy, Laura and Fi. Thanks, too, to David, for the trust he showed by appointing me when I had none of the things listed in the job advert; I hope that faith has been shown to be well placed. Thanks to all at Orbital Towers who have supported me to keep those plates spinning, especially Karl and Andy.

It has been fascinating to enter and learn about a world, publishing, about which previously I knew nothing. Many people have guided me through this labour of love, for the best part of four years. Thanks initially to various people at HC, for all the time and effort you put in, especially Zoe and Nira. Of late, it has been the incredible staff at Biteback, whose talent, insight and knowledge are truly world-class: my thanks to Olivia and James for believing in me and in this book, and guiding me through the past few months, and to David, Vicky and Suzanne.

Huge, heartfelt thanks to the brilliant Iain Dale, for giving me air time, and for giving me the hope and the help that has enabled this book to come to the shelves. If only you agreed with me about school uniform!

Two last special mentions from anonymous times: to 'Charlotte', whose positivity, enthusiasm, encouragement, warmth and all-round loveliness not only made this start to happen but helped me to believe in the aim and purpose of this book; and to RK, who taught me so much about her world and to whom I am indebted, for her brilliant advice, her kindness, her professionalism, her insight, her wit and wisdom and for keeping me going when giving up seemed very, very tempting.

And to the Sicilian Man, for always looking interested when I talk school for hours over dinner, and for keeping my glass topped up.

ABOUT THE AUTHOR

Alison Colwell, originally styled 'The Secret Head Teacher' until the *Sunday Times* blew her cover in an interview in 2020, has spent several decades in teaching. She has held senior leadership positions across a number of schools, including Ebbsfleet Academy in Swanscombe. Under her leadership, Ebbsfleet succeeded in turning around its reputation, resulting in an Ofsted report judging the school 'Good'. Alison now lives and works in Mallorca.

320PP HARDBACK, £16.99

'Twenty-five years a teacher. I could have committed a double murder and been out by now.'

Ever wondered what life is really like for today's teachers? Reasoning that it's either laugh or cry, this author does both while intoning a mantra of 'July, July, July' and praying for a minor heart attack in return for a foot in the door to early retirement. From fending off inspectors to dealing with the alarming rise in mental health issues and increasing alienation of young people, it's fair to say the job has never been more difficult.

Written by an anonymous author working in a state secondary school, this uproariously funny, desperately necessary book takes us inside the classroom to see morale at rock-bottom and a system on its knees. Hilarious, heartbreaking and impassioned, *Class War* is about the importance of good schools and talented teachers at a time when they have never been more essential. Painting a heartfelt portrait of the profession and an education system where no one should be left behind but too many are, this book reveals there is laughter to be found even as a river of effluent is sluicing down the pipe.